A YANKEE

IN THE TRENCHES

By

R. DERBY HOLMES

CORPORAL OF THE 22D LONDON BATTALION
OF THE
QUEEN'S ROYAL WEST SURREY REGIMENT

ILLUSTRATED FROM PHOTOGRAPHS

1918

British Library Cataloguing-in-Publication Data
A catalogue record for this book is available from the
British Library

CONTENTS

A YANKEE

IN THE TRENCHES

LIST OF ILLUSTRATIONS

Introduction to the
World War One Centenary Series

The First World War was a global war centred in Europe that began on 28 July 1914 and lasted until 11 November 1918. More than nine million combatants were killed, a casualty rate exacerbated by the belligerents' technological and industrial sophistication – and tactical stalemate. It was one of the deadliest conflicts in history, paving the way for major political changes, including revolutions in many of the nations involved. The war drew in all the world's great economic powers, which were assembled in two opposing alliances: the Allies (based on the Triple Entente of the United Kingdom, France and the Russian Empire) and the Central Powers of Germany and Austria-Hungary. These alliances were both reorganised and expanded as more nations entered the war: Italy, Japan and the United States joined the Allies, and the Ottoman Empire and Bulgaria joined the Central Powers. Ultimately, more than 70 million military personnel were mobilised.

The war was triggered by the assassination of Archduke Franz Ferdinand of Austria, heir to the throne of Austria-Hungary, by a Yugoslav nationalist, Gavrilo Princip in Sarajevo, June 28th 1914. This set off a diplomatic crisis when Austria-Hungary delivered an ultimatum to Serbia, and international alliances were invoked. Within weeks, the major powers were at war and the conflict soon spread around the world. By the end of the war, four major imperial powers; the German, Russian, Austro-Hungarian and Ottoman empires— ceased to exist. The map of Europe was redrawn, with several independent nations restored or created. On peace, the League of Nations formed with the aim of preventing any repetition of such an appalling conflict, encouraging cooperation and communication between the newly autonomous nation states. This laudatory pursuit failed spectacularly with the advent of the Second World War however, with new European nationalism and the rise of fascism paving the way for the next global crisis.

This book is part of the World War One Centenary series; creating, collating and reprinting new and old works of poetry, fiction, autobiography and analysis. The series forms a commemorative tribute to mark the passing of one of the world's bloodiest wars, offering new perspectives on this tragic yet fascinating period of human history.

Amelia Carruthers

A Timeline of the Major Events of World War One in Europe

1914

28th June   Franz Ferdinand Assassinated at Sarajevo.

29th June   Austro-Hungary send despatch to Vienna accusing Serbian complicity in the killing.

5th July   Kaiser Wilhelm promises German support for Austria against Serbia.

20th July   Austria-Hungary sends troops to the Serbian frontier.

25th July   Serbia mobilises its troops, Russia sends troops to the Austrian frontier.

28th July   Austria-Hungary Declares war on Serbia.

29th July	Austrians bombard Belgrade and German patrols cross the French border. Britain warns it cannot remain neutral.
1st August	Germany declares war on Russia. Italy and Belgium announce neutrality. French mobilisation ordered.
3rd August	Germany declares war on France and invades Belgium (Schlieffen plan). Great Britain mobilises.
4th August	Britain declares war on Germany and Austria-Hungary (after ultimatum to stand down). US declares neutrality. Germany declares war on Belgium.
6th August	First British casualties with the HMS Amphion sunk by German mines in the North sea. 150 men dead.
7th August	First members of the BEF (British Expeditionary Force) arrive in France.

11th August	Start of enlisting for Kitchener's New Army 'Your King and Country Need You'.
20th August	Brussels is evacuated as German troops occupy the city.
23rd August	The BEF started its retreat from Mons. Germany invades France.
26th August	Russian army defeated at Tannenburg and Masurian Lakes. BEF suffers over 7000 casualties at the Battle of Le Cateau –forced to retreat.
6th September	Battle of the Marne starts; checks German advance, but at the cost of 13,000 British, 250,000 French and 250,000 German casualties.
19th October	First Battle of Ypres.
29th October	Turkey enters the war (on Germany's side).
22nd November	Trenches are now established along the entire Western Front.
8th December	Battle of the Falkland Islands.

1915

19th January	First Zeppelin raid on Britain (Great Yarmouth and Kings Lynn – killing 5).
18th February	Blockade of Great Britain by German U-boats begins. All vessels considered viable targets, including neutrals.
22nd April	Second Battle of Ypres begins. Widespread use of poison gas by Germany.
25th April	Allied troops land in Gallipoli.
2nd May	Austro-German offensive on Galicia begins.
7th May	The Lusitania is sunk by a German U-Boat – creating US/German diplomatic crisis.
23rd May	Italy declares war on Germany and Austria
31st May	First Zeppelin raid on London, killing 35 and shaking morale.

30th June	German troops use flamethrowers for the first time, against the British at Hooge, Ypres.
5th August	Germany captures Warsaw from the Russians.
21st August	Final British offensive in the Dardanelles (Scimitar Hill, Gallipoli). They lose, and suffer 5000 deaths.
25th September	Start of the Battle of Loos and Champagne. The British use gas for the first time, but the wind blows it over their own troops, resulting in 2632 casualties.
31st October	Steel helmets introduced on the British Front.
15th December	Sir Douglas Haig replaces Sir John French as Commander of the BEF.

1916

8th January   Allied evacuation of Helles marks the end of the Gallipoli campaign.

21st February   Start of the Battle of Verdun – German offensive against the Mort-Homme Ridge. The battle lasts 10 months and over a million men become casualties. (Finishes 18th December, the longest and costliest battle of the Western Front).

9th March   Germany declares war on Portugal. Six days later, Austria follows suit.

31st May   Battle of Jutland – lasts until 1st June. German High Seas Fleet is forced to retire despite having inflicted heavier losses on the Royal Navy (14 ships and 6,100 men). German fleet irreparably damaged.

4th June   Start of the Russian Brusilov Offensive on the Eastern front. Nearly cripples Austro-Hungary.

1st July	Start of the Battle of the Somme – 750,000 allied soldiers along a 25 mile front. Nearly 60,000 are dead or wounded on the first day.
14th July	Battle of Bazetin Ridge marks the end of the first Somme Offensive. The British break the German line but fail to deploy cavalry fast enough to take advantage. 9,000 men are lost.
23rd July	Battle of Pozières Ridge marks the second Somme Offensive, costs 17,000 allied casualties – the majority of whom are Australian. (ends 7th August).
10th August	End of the Brusilov Offensive.
9th September	The Battle of Ginchy. The British capture Ginchy – a post of vital strategic importance as it commands a view of the whole battlefield.
15th September	First use en masse of tanks at the Somme. The Battle of Flers-Courcelette signifies the start of the third stage of the Somme offensive.

13th November	Battle of Ancre. The fourth phase of the Somme Offensive is marked by the British capturing Beaumont Hamel and St. Pierre Division, taking nearly 4,000 prisoners.
12th December	Germany delivers Peace Note to Allies suggesting compromise.

1917

1st February | Germany's unrestricted submarine warfare campaign starts.

3rd February | US sever diplomatic relations with Germany as U-boats threaten US shipping. Intercepted messages reveal that Germany is provoking the Mexicans into war with the US.

21st February | The great German withdrawal begins. Serre, Miraumont, Petit Miraumont, Pys and Warlencourt are evacuated, falling back 25 miles to establish stronger positions on the Hindenburg Line.

15th March | Tsar Nicholas II abdicates as Moscow falls to Russian Revolutionaries. Demise of the Russian army frees German troops for the Western front.

6th April | USA declares war on Germany – troops mobilise immediately.

9th April	Battle of Arras. British successfully employ new tactics of creeping barrages, the 'graze fuse' and counter battery fire.
16th April	France launches an unsuccessful offensive on the Western Front. – Second Battle of Aisne begins as part of the 'Nivelle Offensive'. Losses are horrendous, triggering mutinies in the French Army.
7th June	The Battle of Messines Ridge. British succeed with few casualties, detonating 19 mines under German front lines – the explosions are reportedly heard from England.
13th June	Germans launch first major heavy bomber raid of London – kills and injures 594.
25th June	First US troops arrive in France.
31st July	Start of the Third Battle at Ypres – a 15 mile front in Flanders. Initial attacks are successful as the German forward trenches are lightly manned.

15th August	The Battle of Lens (Hill 70). – Canadians at the forefront , won a high vantage point, though loss of 9,200 men.
20th August	Third Battle of Verdun begins. French progress is marked by gaining lost territory in the earlier battles.
9th October	The third phase of the Ypres Offensive begins with British and French troops taking Poelcapelle. 25mm of rain falls in 48 hours and the battlefield turns into a quagmire.
12th October	British launch assault at Ypres Against the Passchendale Ridge. New Zealand and Australians take terrible casualties. Bogged down in mud and forced back to start lines.
24th October	Battle of Caporetto – Italian Army heavily defeated.
26th October	Second Battle of Passchendaele begins, 12,000 men lost and 300 yards gained (ends 10th November – 500,000 casualties,

140,000 deaths and 5 miles gained).

6th November	Britain launches major offensive on the Western Front.
20th November	Victory for British tanks at Cambrai - The Royal flying Corps drop bombs at the same time on German anti-tank guns and strong points. Early example of the 'Blitzkrieg' tactics later used by Germany in World War Two.
5th December	Armistice between Germany and Russia signed.

1918

16th January   Riots in Vienna and Budapest with dissatisfaction at the war.

3rd March   Treaty of Brest-Litovsk signed between (Soviet) Russia and Germany.

21st March   Second Battle of the Somme marked by the German spring offensive, the 'Kaiserschlacht'. Germans attack along a 50 mile front south of Arras.

22nd March   Victory for Germany with operation Michael - Use of new 'Storm trooper' assault to smash through British positions west of St. Quentin, taking 16,000 prisoners.

23rd March   Greatest air battle of the war takes place over the Somme, with 70 aircraft involved.

5th April   The German Spring Offensive halts outside Amiens as British and Australian forces hold the Line. The second 1917 battle of

	the Somme ends, as Germany calls off operation Michael.
9th April	Germany starts offensive in Flanders –Battle of the Lys (ends 29th April).
19th May	German air force launches largest raid on London, using 33 aircraft.
27th May	Operation Blucher – The Third German Spring Offensive attacks the French army along the Aisne River. French are forced back to the Marne, but hold the river with help from the Americans.
15th July	Second battle of the Marne started; final phase of German spring offensive. Start of the collapse of the German army with irreplaceable casualties.
8th August	Second Battle of Amiens – German resistance sporadic and thousands surrender.
27th September	British offensive on the Cambrai Front leads to the storming of the Hindenburg Line. Battle of St.

Quentin – British and U.S troops launch devastating offensives.

4th October	Germany asks the allies for an armistice (sent to Woodrow Wilson).

4th October — Germany asks the allies for an armistice (sent to Woodrow Wilson).

8th October — Allies advance along a 20 mile front from St. Quentin to Cambrai, driving the Germans back and capturing 10,000 troops.

29th October — Germany's navy mutinies (at Jade).

3rd November — Austria makes peace. German sailors mutiny at Kiel.

9th November — Kaiser Wilhelm abdicates and revolution breaks out in Berlin.

11th November — Germany signs the armistice with the allies – coming into effect at 11.00am (official end of WWI).

1919

10th January	Communist Revolt in Berlin (Battle of Berlin).
18th January	Paris Peace Conference Begins.
25th January	Principle of a League of Nations ratified.
6th May	Under conditions of the Peace conference, German colonies are annexed.
21st June	The surrendered German naval fleet at Scapa Flow was scuttled.
28th June	Treaty of Versailles signed.
19th July	Cenotaph unveiled in London.

By Amelia Carruthers

Memoirs, Diaries and Poems of World War One

In 1939, the writer Robert Graves was asked to write an article for the BBC's *Listener* magazine, explaining 'as a war poet of the last war, why so little poetry has so far been produced by this one.' From the very first weeks of fighting, the First World War inspired enormous amounts of poetry, factual analysis, autobiography and fiction - from all countries involved in the conflict. 2,225 English war poets have been counted, of whom 1808 were civilians. The 'total' nature of this war perhaps goes someway to explaining its enormous impact on the popular imagination. Even today, commemorations and the effects of a 'lost generation' are still being witnessed. It was a war fought for traditional, nationalistic values of the nineteenth century, propagated using twentieth century technological and industrial methods of killing. Memoirs, diaries and poems provide extraordinary insight into how the common soldier experienced everyday life in the trenches, and how the civilian population dealt with this loss.

Over two thousand published poets wrote about the war, yet only a small fraction are still known today. Many that were popular with contemporary readers are now obscure. The selection, which emerged as orthodox during the 1960s, tends to (understandably) emphasise the horror of war, suffering, tragedy and anger against those that wage war. This was not entirely the case however, as demonstrated in the early weeks of the war. British poets responded with an outpouring of patriotic literary production. Robert Bridges, Poet Laureate, contributed a poem *Wake Up England!* calling for 'Thou careless, awake! Thou peacemaker, fight! Stand, England, for honour, And God guard the Right!' He later wished the work to be suppressed though. Rudyard Kipling's *For All We Have and Are,* aroused the most comment however, with its references to the 'Hun at the gate... the crazed and driven foe.'

From Hemingway's *A Farewell to Arms,* to Remarque's *All Quiet on the Western Front,* to the poetry of Sassoon, Graves, and Brooke, there are numerous examples of acclaimed writing inspired by the Great War. One of the best known war poets is perhaps Wilfred Owen, killed in battle at the age of twenty-five. His poems written at the front achieved popular attention soon after the war's end, most famously including *Dulce Et Decorum Est, Anthem for Doomed Youth,* and *Strange Meeting.* In preparing for the publication of his collected poems, Owen explained 'This book is not about heroes. English poetry is not yet fit to speak of them. Nor is it about deeds, or lands, nor anything about glory, honour, might, majesty, dominion, or power, except War. Above all I am not concerned with Poetry. My subject is War, and the pity of War. The Poetry is in the pity.'

Dulce et Decorum Est, one of Owen's most famous poems, scathingly takes Horace's statement, 'Dulce et decorum est, pro patria mori', meaning 'It is sweet and proper to die for one's country' as its title. It chiefly describes the death of an anonymous soldier due to poison gas, vividly describing the suffering of the man, ending with a bitter attack on those who see glory in the death of others. Such themes were also widely utilised by authors unaccustomed with the literary canon - the common soldier noting down their experiences for their loved ones, and for posterity. Each unit in World War One was in fact required to keep a diary of its day-to-day activities, many portraying the anxiety and terror of the opening days of the war. Diaries from soldiers in the First Battalion South Wales Borderers (among others, recently released at the British National Archives) described the battles of the Marne and the Aisne, with one captain who said the scenes he witnesses were 'beyond description... poor fellows shot dead are lying in all directions... everywhere the same hard, grim pitiless sign of battle and war. I have had a belly full of it.'

Other, lighter aspects of everyday life including tugs of war, rugby matches and farewell dinners to mark the end of the fighting have also been documented, giving us a rare insight into what the First World War was like for the men on the front line. Letters were an incredibly important part of life as a soldier. Receiving and writing them helped keep them sane, and could take them away from the realities of trench life. Every week, an average of 12.5 million letters were sent to soldiers by family, friends, and partners. More formalised memoirs have also become a key way of understanding the conflict, from gas attacks, the fear of going over the top, methods of coping with death - as well as the jovial camaraderie which often grew up between the men. The first memoirs of combatants were published in 1922, not long after the armistice: *A Tank Driver's Experiences* by Arthur Jenkins and *Disenchantment* by Charles Edward Montague. These were shortly joined with *Good-Bye to All That* (1929) by Robert Graves, *A Subaltern's War* (1929) by Charles Edmund Carrington, and *Blasting and Bombardiering* (1937) byPercy Wyndham Lewis. Nurses also published memoirs of their wartime experiences, such as *A Diary without Dates* (1918) by Enid Bagnold, and *Forbidden Zone* (1929) by Mary Borden. Vera Brittain's *Testament of Youth* (first published 1933) has been acclaimed as a classic for its description of the impact of the war on the lives of women and the civilian population - extending into the post-war years.

Storm of Steel, written by Ernst Jünger, published in 1920 was one of the first personal accounts to be published - a graphic account of trench warfare, unusually glorifying the sacrifice encountered. The book has consequently been criticised for lionizing war, especially when compared with works such as Remarque's (albeit fictional) *All Quiet on the Western Front.* In the preface to the 1929 English edition, Jünger stated that; 'Time only strengthens my conviction that it was a good and strenuous life, and that the war, for all its destructiveness, was an incomparable schooling of the heart.' As is evident from this short introduction to the memoirs, diaries, letters and poems of the first world war

- it is an intensely complex field. Dependent on military rank, geographic position and placement, nationality and subjective experience and character, they take on a wide variety of forms and focuses. Such works give an amazing insight into the experiences of combatants and it is hoped the current reader is encouraged to find out more about this thoroughly worthwhile topic.

Amelia Carruthers

Image 1. British soldiers at chow in the trenches

The Western Front

The First World War was one of the deadliest conflicts in history. More than seven million civilians and nine million combatants were killed, a casualty rate exacerbated by the belligerents' technological and industrial sophistication – and tactical stalemate. It lasted four years, however nobody expected the war to be more than a short, decisive battle. Following the outbreak of war in 1914, the German Army opened the Western Front by first invading Luxembourg and Belgium, then gaining military control of important industrial regions in France. Battle raged until the end of the war in 1918 when the German government sued for peace, unable to sustain the massive losses suffered. The western front included some of the bloodiest conflicts of the war, with few significant advances made; among the most costly of these offensives were the Battle of Verdun with a combined 700,000 dead, the Battle of the Somme with more than a million casualties, and the Battle of Passchendaele with roughly 600,000 casualties.

The massive tide of initial German advance was only turned with the Battle of the Marne, when the German army came within 70km of Paris. This, first battle of the Marne (5th-12th September 1914) enabled French and British troops to force the German retreat by exploiting a gap which appeared between the first and second Armies. The German army retreated north of the Aisne River and dug in there, establishing the beginnings of a static western front that was to last for the next three years.

Following this German setback, the opposing forces tried to outflank each other in the Race for the Sea, and quickly extended their trench systems from the North Sea to the Swiss frontier. As a result of this frenzied race, both sides dug in along a meandering line of fortified trenches, stretching all the way along the front - a line which remained essentially unchanged for most of the war.

Between 1915 and 1917 there were several major offensives along this front. The attacks employed massive artillery bombardments and massed infantry advances. However, a combination of entrenchments, machine gun nests, barbed wire, and artillery repeatedly inflicted severe casualties on the attackers and counterattacking defenders. In an effort to break the deadlock, the western front saw the introduction of new military technology, including poison gas, aircraft and tanks. Although all sides had signed treaties (the Hague Conventions of 1899 and 1907) which prohibited the use of chemical weapons in warfare, they were used on a large scale during the conflict. This was most evident at the Second Battle of Ypres (21 April – 25 May 1915), an offensive led by the Germans in order to disrupt Franco-British planning and test a relatively new weapon; chlorine gas. The Germans released 168 tons of this gas onto the battlefield, creating panic amongst the British soldiers - many of whom fled creating an undefended 6km wide gap in the Allied line.

The Germans were unprepared for the level of their success however and lacked sufficient reserves to exploit the opening. Canadian troops quickly arrived and drove back the German advance. It was only after the adoption of substantially revised tactics that some degree of mobility was restored to the front. The German Spring Offensive of put such ideas to good use, with recently introduced infiltration tactics, involving small, lightly equipped infantry forces attacking enemy rear areas while bypassing enemy front line strong-points and isolating them for attack by follow-up troops with heavier weapons. They advanced nearly 97km to the west, which marked the deepest advance by either side since 1914 and very nearly succeeded in forcing a breakthrough. The German Chief of Staff, Erich von Falkenhayn, believed that a breakthrough might no longer be possible, and instead focused on forcing a French capitulation by inflicting massive casualties. The new goal was to 'bleed France white.'

This policy resulted in the Battle of Verdun, which began on 21st February after a nine-day delay due to snow and blizzards. To inflict the maximum possible casualties, Falkenhayn planned to attack a position from which the French could not retreat for reason of both strategic positions and national pride - Verdun was an important stronghold, surrounded by a ring of forts, guarding the direct route to Paris. The French put up heavy resistance though, and halted the German advance by 28th February. Over the summer they slowly advanced with the use of the rolling barrages and pushed the Germans back 2km from their original position. This battle, known as the 'Mincing Machine of Verdun' became a symbol of French determination and self-sacrifice. The futility and mass slaughter of the war was perhaps nowhere better illustrated than in the Battle of the Somme however; convened to help relieve the French after their enormous losses at Verdun.

Here, British divisions in Picardy launched an attack around the river Somme, supported by five French divisions on their right flank. The attack was preceded by seven days of heavy artillery bombardment, which failed to destroy any of the German defences. This resulted in the greatest number of casualties (killed, wounded, and missing) in a single day in the history of the British army, about 57,000. By August 1916, General Haig, like Falkenhayn, concluded that a breakthrough was unlikely, and instead switched tactics to a series of small unit actions (similar to the German infiltration tactics). The final phase of the Somme also saw the first use of the tank on the battlefield, which did make early progress (4km), but they were mechanically unreliable and ultimately failed. All told, the battle which lasted five months only succeeded in advancing eight kilometres, at a truly massive loss to life. The British had suffered about 420,000 casualties and the French around 200,000. It is estimated that the Germans lost 465,000, although this figure is controversial.

This constant loss of life meant that troop morale became incredibly low. The Nivelle Offensive, primarily including French and Russian troops - which promised to end the war within forty-eight hours, was significant failure. It took place on rough, upward sloping terrain, tiring the men - whose troubles were increased due to poor intelligence and German control of the skies. Within a week, 100,000 French troops were dead and on 3rd May, an entire division refused their orders to march, arriving drunk and without their weapons. Mutinies then spread and afflicted a further fifty-four French divisions, only stopped by mass arrests and trials. Such low morale was further dampened by the German's final spring offensives which very nearly succeeded in driving the allies apart

Operation Michael (March 1918), the first of these German offensives advanced 100 km, getting within shelling distance of Paris for the first time since 1914. The allies responded with vigour however, with a counter-offensive at the Marne, followed by an attack at Amiens to the North. This attack included Franco-British forces, and was spearheaded by Australian and Canadian troops, along with 600 tanks and supported by 800 aircraft. The assault proved highly successful, leading Hindenburg to name 8 August as the 'Black Day of the German Army.' These losses persuaded the German government to sue for armistice, and the Hundred Days Offensive (beginning in August 1918) proved the final straw. Many German troops surrendered, although fighting did continue until the armistice was signed on 11th November 1918. The war in the Western Front's trenches left a generation of maimed soldiers and grieved populations, though proved a decisive theatre in ending the First World War. The repercussions of this bloody conflict are still being felt to this day. It is hoped the current reader is encouraged to find out more, and enjoys this book.

Amelia Carruthers

In Flanders Fields

In Flanders fields the poppies blow
Between the crosses, row on row,
That mark our place; and in the sky
The larks, still bravely singing, fly
Scarce heard amid the guns below.

We are the Dead. Short days ago
We lived, felt dawn, saw sunset glow,
Loved and were loved, and now we lie
In Flanders fields.

Take up our quarrel with the foe:
To you from failing hands we throw
The torch; be yours to hold it high.
If ye break faith with us who die
We shall not sleep, though poppies grow
In Flanders fields.

John McCrae, May 1915

The War was decided in the first twenty days of fighting, and all that happened afterwards consisted in battles which, however formidable and devastating, were but desperate and vain appeals against the decision of Fate.

Winston Churchill (1874–1965), British statesman, writer. Liaison 1914, preface, E.L. Spears (1930).

A YANKEE

IN THE TRENCHES

CORPORAL HOLMES IN THE UNIFORM OF THE 22ND LONDON
BATTALION, QUEEN'S ROYAL WEST SURREY REGIMENT,
H. M. IMPERIAL ARMY. *Frontispiece.*

34

Dedication

TO MARION A. PUTTEE, SOUTHALL,
MIDDLESEX, ENGLAND, I DEDICATE THIS
BOOK AS A TOKEN OF APPRECIATION FOR ALL
THE LOVING THOUGHTS AND DEEDS
BESTOWED UPON ME WHEN I WAS A
STRANGER IN A STRANGE LAND

FOREWORD

I have tried as an American in writing this book to give the public a complete view of the trenches and life on the Western Front as it appeared to me, and also my impression of conditions and men as I found them. It has been a pleasure to write it, and now that I have finished I am genuinely sorry that I cannot go further. On the lecture tour I find that people ask me questions, and I have tried in this book to give in detail many things about the quieter side of war that to an audience would seem too tame. I feel that the public want to know how the soldiers live when not in the trenches, for all the time out there is not spent in killing and carnage. As in the case of all men in the trenches, I heard things and stories that especially impressed me, so I have written them as hearsay, not taking to myself credit as their originator. I trust that the reader will find as much joy in the cockney character as I did and which I have tried to show the public; let me say now that no finer body of men than those Bermondsey boys of my battalion could be found.

I think it fair to say that in compiling the trench terms at the end of this book I have not copied any war book, but I have given in each case my own version of the words, though I will confess that the idea and necessity of having such a list sprang from reading Sergeant Empey's "Over the Top." It would be impossible to write a book that the people would understand without the aid of such a glossary.

It is my sincere wish that after reading this book the reader may have a clearer conception of what this great world war means and what our soldiers are contending with, and that it may awaken the American people to the danger of Prussianism so that when in the future there is a call for funds for Liberty Loans, Red Cross work, or Y.M.C.A., there will be no slacking, for they form the real triangular sign to a successful termination of this terrible conflict.

R. DERBY HOLMES.

A YANKEE IN THE TRENCHES

CHAPTER I

JOINING THE BRITISH ARMY

Once, on the Somme in the fall of 1916, when I had been over the top and was being carried back somewhat disfigured but still in the ring, a cockney stretcher bearer shot this question at me:

"Hi sye, Yank. Wot th' bloody 'ell are you in this bloomin' row for? Ayen't there no trouble t' 'ome?"

And for the life of me I couldn't answer. After more than a year in the British service I could not, on the spur of the moment, say exactly why I was there.

To be perfectly frank with myself and with the reader I had no very lofty motives when I took the King's shilling. When the great war broke out, I was mildly sympathetic with England, and mighty sorry in an indefinite way for France and Belgium; but my sympathies were not strong enough in any direction to get me into uniform with a chance of being killed. Nor, at first, was I able to work up any compelling hate for

Germany. The abstract idea of democracy did not figure in my calculations at all.

However, as the war went on, it became apparent to me, as I suppose it must have to everybody, that the world was going through one of its epochal upheavals; and I figured that with so much history in the making, any unattached young man would be missing it if he did not take a part in the big game.

I had the fondness for adventure usual in young men. I liked to see the wheels go round. And so it happened that, when the war was about a year and a half old, I decided to get in before it was too late.

On second thought I won't say that it was purely love for adventure that took me across. There may have been in the back of my head a sneaking extra fondness for France, perhaps instinctive, for I was born in Paris, although my parents were American and I was brought to Boston as a baby and have lived here since.

Whatever my motives for joining the British army, they didn't have time to crystallize until I had been wounded and sent to Blighty, which is trench slang for England. While recuperating in one of the pleasant places of the English country-side, I had time to acquire a perspective and to discover that I had been fighting for democracy and the future safety of the world. I think that my experience in this respect is like that of most of the young Americans who have volunteered for service under a foreign flag.

I decided to get into the big war game early in 1916. My first thought was to go into the ambulance service, as I knew several men in that work. One of them described the driver's life about as follows. He said:

"The *blessés* curse you because you jolt them. The doctors curse you because you don't get the *blessés* in fast enough. The Transport Service curse you because you get in the way. You eat standing up and don't sleep at all. You're as likely as anybody to get killed, and all the glory you get is the War Cross, if you're lucky, and you don't get a single chance to kill a Hun."

That settled the ambulance for me. I hadn't wanted particularly to kill a Hun until it was suggested that I mightn't. Then I wanted to slaughter a whole division.

So I decided on something where there would be fighting. And having decided, I thought I would "go the whole hog" and work my way across to England on a horse transport.

One day in the first part of February I went, at what seemed an early hour, to an office on Commercial Street, Boston, where they were advertising for horse tenders for England. About three hundred men were earlier than I. It seemed as though every beach-comber and patriot in New England was trying to get across. I didn't get the job, but filed my application and was lucky enough to be signed on for a sailing on February 22 on the steam-ship *Cambrian*, bound for London.

REDUCED FACSIMILE OF DISCHARGE CERTIFICATE OF CHARACTER.

We spent the morning of Washington's Birthday loading the horses. These government animals were selected stock and full of ginger. They seemed to know that they were going to France and resented it keenly. Those in my care seemed to regard my attentions as a personal affront.

We had a strenuous forenoon getting the horses aboard, and sailed at noon. After we had herded in the livestock, some of the officers herded up the herders. I drew a pink slip with two numbers on it, one showing the compartment where I was supposed to sleep, the other indicating my bunk.

That compartment certainly was a glory-hole. Most of the men had been drunk the night before, and the place had the rich, balmy fragrance of a water-front saloon. Incidentally there was a good deal of unauthorized and undomesticated livestock. I made a limited acquaintance with that pretty, playful little creature, the "cootie," who was to become so familiar in the trenches later on. He wasn't called a cootie aboard ship, but he was the same bird.

Perhaps the less said about that trip across the better. It lasted twenty-one days. We fed the animals three times a day and cleaned the stalls once on the trip. I got chewed up some and stepped on a few times. Altogether the experience was good intensive training for the trench life to come; especially the bunks. Those sleeping quarters sure were close and crawly.

We landed in London on Saturday night about nine-thirty. The immigration inspectors gave us a quick examination and we were turned back to the shipping people, who paid us off,—two pounds, equal to about ten dollars real change.

After that we rode on the train half an hour and then marched through the streets, darkened to fool the Zeps. Around one o'clock we brought up at Thrawl Street, at the lodgings where we were supposed to stop until we were started for home.

The place where we were quartered was a typical London doss house. There were forty beds in the room with mine, all of them occupied. All hands were snoring, and the fellow in the next cot was going it with the cut-out wide open, breaking all records. Most of the beds sagged like a hammock. Mine humped up in the middle like a pile of bricks.

I was up early and was directed to the place across the way where we were to eat. It was labeled "Mother Wolf's. The Universal Provider." She provided just one meal of weak tea, moldy bread, and rancid bacon for me. After that I went to a hotel. I may remark in passing that horse tenders, going or coming or in between whiles, do not live on the fat of the land.

I spent the day—it was Sunday—seeing the sights of Whitechapel, Middlesex Street or Petticoat Lane, and some of the slums. Next morning it was pretty clear to me that two pounds don't go far in the big town. I promptly boarded the first bus for Trafalgar Square. The recruiting office was just down the road in Whitehall at the old Scotland Yard office.

I had an idea when I entered that recruiting office that the sergeant would receive me with open arms. He didn't. Instead he looked me over with unqualified scorn and spat out, "Yank, ayen't ye?"

And I in my innocence briefly answered, "Yep."

"We ayen't tykin' no nootrals," he said, with a sneer. And then: "Better go back to Hamerika and 'elp Wilson write 'is blinkin' notes."

Well, I was mad enough to poke that sergeant in the eye. But I didn't. I retired gracefully and with dignity.

At the door another sergeant hailed me, whispering behind his hand, "Hi sye, mytie. Come around in the mornin'. Hi'll get ye in." And so it happened.

Next day my man was waiting and marched me boldly up to the same chap who had refused me the day before.

"'Ere's a recroot for ye, Jim," says my friend.

Jim never batted an eye. He began to "awsk" questions and to fill out a blank. When he got to the birthplace, my guide cut in and said, "Canada."

The only place I knew in Canada was Campobello Island, a place where we camped one summer, and I gave that. I don't think that anything but rabbits was ever born on Campobello, but it went. For that matter anything went. I discovered afterward that the sergeant who had captured me on the street got five bob (shillings) for me.

The physical examination upstairs was elaborate. They told me to strip, weighed me, and said I was fit. After that I was taken in to an officer—a real officer this time—who made me put my hand on a Bible and say yes to an oath he rattled off. Then he told me I was a member of the Royal Fusiliers, gave me two shillings, sixpence and ordered me to report at the Horse Guards Parade next day. I was in the British army,—just like that!

I spent the balance of the day seeing the sights of London, and incidentally spending my coin. When I went around to the Horse Guards next morning, two hundred others, new rookies like myself, were waiting. An officer gave me another two shillings, sixpence. I began to think that if the money kept coming along at that rate the British army might turn out a good investment. It didn't.

That morning I was sent out to Hounslow Barracks, and three days later was transferred to Dover with twenty others. I was at Dover a little more than two months and completed my training there.

Our barracks at Dover was on the heights of the cliffs, and on clear days we could look across the Channel and see the dim outlines of France. It was a fascination for all of us to look away over there and to wonder what fortunes were to come to us on the battle fields of Europe. It was perhaps as well that none of us had imagination enough to visualize the things that were ahead.

I found the rookies at Dover a jolly, companionable lot, and I never found the routine irksome. We were up at five-thirty, had cocoa and biscuits, and then an hour of physical drill or bayonet practice. At eight came breakfast of tea, bacon, and bread, and then we drilled until twelve. Dinner. Out again on the parade ground until three thirty. After that we were free.

Nights we would go into Dover and sit around the "pubs" drinking ale, or "ayle" as the cockney says it.

After a few weeks, when we were hardened somewhat, they began to inflict us with the torture known as "night ops." That means going out at ten o'clock under full pack, hiking several miles, and then "manning" the trenches around the town and returning to barracks at three A.M.

This wouldn't have been so bad if we had been excused parades the following day. But no. We had the same old drills except the early one, but were allowed to "kip" until seven.

In the two months I completed the musketry course, was a good bayonet man, and was well grounded in bombing practice. Besides that I was as hard as nails and had learned thoroughly the system of British discipline.

I had supposed that it took at least six months to make a soldier,—in fact had been told that one could not be turned out who would be ten per cent efficient in less than that time. That old theory is all wrong. Modern warfare changes so fast that the only thing that can be taught a man is the basic principles of discipline, bombing, trench warfare, and musketry. Give him those things, a well-conditioned body, and a baptism of fire, and he will be right there with the veterans, doing his bit.

Two months was all our crowd got at any rate, and they were as good as the best, if I do say it.

My training ended abruptly with a furlough of five days for Embarkation Leave, that is, leave before going to France. This is a sort of good-by vacation. Most fellows realize fully that it may be their last look at Blighty, and they take it rather solemnly. To a stranger without friends in England I can imagine that this Embarkation Leave would be either a mighty lonesome, dismal affair, or a stretch of desperate, homesick dissipation. A chap does want to say good-by to some one before he goes away, perhaps to die. He wants to be loved and to have some one sorry that he is going.

I was invited by one of my chums to spend the leave with him at his home in Southall, Middlesex. His father, mother and sister welcomed me in a way that made me know it was my home from the minute I entered the door. They took me into their hearts with a simple hospitality and whole-souled kindness that I can never forget. I was a stranger in a strange land and they made me one of their own. I shall never be able to repay all the loving thoughts and deeds of that family and shall remember them while I live. My chum's mother I call Mother too. It is to her that I have dedicated this book.

After my delightful few days of leave, things moved fast. I was back in Dover just two days when I, with two hundred other men, was sent to Winchester. Here we were notified that we were transferred to the Queen's Royal West Surrey Regiment.

This news brought a wild howl from the men. They wanted to stop with the Fusiliers. It is part of the British system that every man is taught the traditions and history of his regiment and to *know* that his is absolutely the best in the whole army. In a surprisingly short time they get so they swear by their own regiment and by their officers, and they protest bitterly at a transfer.

Personally I didn't care a rap. I had early made up my mind that I was a very small pebble on the beach and that it was up to me to obey orders and keep my mouth shut.

On June 17, some eighteen hundred of us were moved down to Southampton and put aboard the transport for Havre. The next day we were in France, at Harfleur, the central training camp outside Havre.

We were supposed to undergo an intensive training at Harfleur in the various forms of gas and protection from it, barbed wire and methods of construction of entanglements, musketry, bombing, and bayonet fighting.

Harfleur was a miserable place. They refused to let us go in town after drill. Also I managed to let myself in for something that would have kept me in camp if town leave had been allowed.

The first day there was a call for a volunteer for musketry instructor. I had qualified and jumped at it. When I reported, an old Scotch sergeant told me to go to the quartermaster for equipment. I said I already had full equipment. Whereupon the sergeant laughed a rumbling Scotch laugh and told me I had to go into kilts, as I was assigned to a Highland contingent.

I protested with violence and enthusiasm, but it didn't do any good. They gave me a dinky little pleated petticoat, and when I demanded breeks to wear underneath, I got the merry ha ha. Breeks on a Scotchman? Never!

Well, I got into the fool things, and I felt as though I was naked from ankle to wishbone. I couldn't get used to the outfit. I am naturally a modest man. Besides, my architecture was never intended for bare-leg effects. I have no dimples in my knees.

So I began an immediate campaign for transfer back to the Surreys. I got it at the end of ten days, and with it came a hurry call from somewhere at the front for more troops.

CHAPTER II

GOING IN

The excitement of getting away from camp and the knowledge that we were soon to get into the thick of the big game pleased most of us. We were glad to go. At least we thought so.

Two hundred of us were loaded into side-door Pullmans, forty to the car. It was a kind of sardine or Boston Elevated effect, and by the time we reached Rouen, twenty-four hours later, we had kinks in our legs and corns on our elbows. Also we were hungry, having had nothing but bully beef and biscuits. We made "char", which is trench slang for tea, in the station, and after two hours moved up the line again, this time in real coaches.

Next night we were billeted at Barlin—don't get that mixed up with Berlin, it's not the same—in an abandoned convent within range of the German guns. The roar of artillery was continuous and sounded pretty close.

Now and again a shell would burst near by with a kind of hollow "spung", but for some reason we didn't seem to mind. I had expected to get the shivers at the first sound of the guns and was surprised when I woke up in the morning after a solid night's sleep.

A message came down from the front trenches at daybreak that we were wanted and wanted quick. We slung together a dixie of char and some bacon and bread for breakfast, and marched around to the "quarters", where they issued "tin hats", extra "ammo", and a second gas helmet. A good many of the men had been out before, and they did the customary "grousing" over the added load.

The British Tommy growls or grouses over anything and everything. He's never happy unless he's unhappy. He resents especially having anything officially added to his pack, and you can't blame him, for in full equipment he certainly is all dressed up like a pack horse.

After the issue we were split up into four lots for the four companies of the battalion, and after some "wangling" I got into Company C, where I stopped all the time I was in France. I was glad, because most of my chums were in that unit.

We got into our packs and started up the line immediately. As we neared the lines we were extended into artillery formation, that is, spread out so that a shell bursting in the road would inflict fewer casualties.

At Bully-Grenay, the point where we entered the communication trenches, guides met us and looked us over, commenting most frankly and freely on our appearance. They didn't seem to think we would amount to much, and said so. They agreed that the "bloomin' Yank" must be a "bloody fool" to come out there. There were times later when I agreed with them.

It began to rain as we entered the communication trench, and I had my first taste of mud. That is literal, for with mud knee-deep in a trench just wide enough for two men to pass you get smeared from head to foot.

Incidentally, as we approached nearer the front, I got my first smell of the dead. It is something you never get away from in the trenches. So many dead have been buried so hastily and so lightly that they are constantly being uncovered by shell bursts. The acrid stench pervades everything, and is so thick you can fairly taste it. It makes nearly everybody deathly sick at first, but one becomes used to it as to anything else.

This communication trench was over two miles long, and it seemed like twenty. We finally landed in a support trench called "Mechanics" (every trench has a name, like a street), and from there into the first-line trench.

I have to admit a feeling of disappointment in that first trench. I don't know what I expected to see, but what I did see was just a long, crooked ditch with a low step running along one side, and with sandbags on top. Here and there was a muddy, bedraggled Tommy half asleep, nursing a dirty and muddy rifle on "sentry go." Everything was very quiet at the moment—no rifles popping, as I had expected, no bullets flying, and, as it happened, absolutely no shelling in the whole sector.

I forgot to say that we had come up by daylight. Ordinarily troops are moved at night, but the communication trench from Bully-Grenay was very deep and was protected at points by little hills, and it was possible to move men in the daytime.

Arrived in the front trench, the sergeant-major appeared, crawling out of his dug-out—the usual place for a sergeant-major—and greeted us with,

"Keep your nappers down, you rooks. Don't look over the top. It ayen't 'ealthy."

It is the regular warning to new men. For some reason the first emotion of the rookie is an overpowering curiosity. He wants to take a peep into No Man's Land. It feels safe enough when things are quiet. But there's always a Fritzie over yonder with a telescope-sighted rifle, and it's about ten to one he'll get you if you stick the old "napper" up in daylight.

The Germans, by the way, have had the "edge" on the Allies in the matter of sniping, as in almost all lines of artillery and musketry practice. The Boche sniper is nearly always armed with a periscope-telescope rifle. This is a specially built super-accurate rifle mounted on a periscope frame. It is thrust up over the parapet and the image of the opposing parapet is cast on a little ground-glass screen on which are two crossed lines. At one hundred fifty yards or less the image is brought up to touching distance seemingly. Fritz simply trains his piece on some low place or anywhere that a head may be expected. When one appears on the screen, he pulls the trigger,—and you "click it" if you happen to be on the other or receiving end. The shooter never shows himself.

I remember the first time I looked through a periscope I had no sooner thrust the thing up than a bullet crashed into the upper mirror, splintering it. Many times I have stuck up a cap on a stick and had it pierced.

The British sniper, on the other hand—at least in my time—had a plain telescope rifle and had to hide himself behind old masonry, tree trunks, or anything convenient, and camouflaged himself in all sorts of ways. At that he was constantly in danger.

I was assigned to Platoon 10 and found they were a good live bunch. Corporal Wells was the best of the lot, and we became fast friends. He helped me learn a lot of my new duties and the trench "lingo", which is like a new language, especially to a Yank.

Wells started right in to make me feel at home and took me along with two others of the new men down to our "apartments", a dug-out built for about four, and housing ten.

My previous idea of a dug-out had been a fairly roomy sort of cave, somewhat damp, but comparatively comfortable. Well, this hole was about four and a half feet high—you had to get in doubled up on your hands and knees—about five by six feet on the sides, and there was no floor, just muck. There was some sodden, dirty straw and a lot of old moldy sandbags. Seven men and their equipment were packed in here, and we made ten.

There was a charcoal brazier going in the middle with two or three mess tins of char boiling away.

Everybody was smoking, and the place stunk to high heaven, or it would have if there hadn't been a bit of burlap over the door.

I crowded up into a corner with my back against the mud wall and my knees under my chin. The men didn't seem overglad to see us, and groused a good deal about the extra crowding. They regarded me with extra disfavor because I was a lance corporal, and they disapproved of any young whipper-snapper just out from Blighty with no trench experience pitchforked in with even a slight superior rank. I had thought up to then that a lance corporal was pretty near as important as a brigadier.

"We'll soon tyke that stripe off ye, me bold lad," said one big cockney.

They were a decent lot after all. Since we were just out from Blighty, they showered us with questions as to how things looked "t' 'ome." And then somebody asked what was the latest song. Right here was where I made my hit and got in right. I sing a bit, and I piped up with the newest thing from the music halls, "Tyke Me Back to Blighty." Here it is:

Tyke me back to dear old Blighty,
Put me on the tryne for London town,
Just tyke me over there

And drop me anywhere,
Manchester, Leeds, or Birmingham,
I don't care.

I want to go see me best gal;
Cuddlin' up soon we'll be,
Hytey iddle de eyety.
Tyke me back to Blighty,
That's the plyce for me.

It doesn't look like much and I'm afraid my rendition of cockney dialect into print isn't quite up to Kipling's. But the song had a pretty little lilting melody, and it went big. They made me sing it about a dozen times and were all joining in at the end.

Then they got sentimental—and gloomy.

"Gawd lumme!" says the big fellow who had threatened my beloved stripes. "Wot a life. Squattin' 'ere in the bloody mud like a blinkin' frog. Fightin' fer wot? Wot, I arsks yer? Gawd lumme! I'd give me bloomin' napper to stroll down the Strand agyne wif me swagger stick an' drop in a private bar an' 'ave me go of 'Aig an' 'Aig."

"Garn," cuts in another Tommy. "Yer blinkin' 'igh wif yer wants, ayen't ye? An' yer 'Aig an' 'Aig. Drop me down in Great Lime Street (Liverpool) an' it's me fer the Golden Sheaf, and a pint of bitter, an' me a 'oldin' 'Arriet's 'and over th' bar. I'm a courtin' 'er when," etc., etc.

And then a fresh-faced lad chirps up: "T' 'ell wif yer Lonnon an' yer whuskey. Gimme a jug o' cider on the sunny side of a 'ay rick in old Surrey. Gimme a happle tart to go wif it. Gawd, I'm fed up on bully beef."

And so it went. All about pubs and bar-maids and the things they'd eat and drink, and all of it Blighty.

They were in the midst of a discussion of what part of the body was most desirable to part with for a permanent Blighty wound when a young officer pushed aside the burlap and wedged in. He was a lieutenant and was in command of our platoon. His name was Blofeld.

Blofeld was most democratic. He shook hands with the new men and said he hoped we'd be live wires, and then he told us what he wanted. There was to be a raid the next night and he was looking for volunteers.

Nobody spoke for a long minute, and then I offered.

I think I spoke more to break the embarrassing silence than anything else. I think, too, that I was led a little by a kind of youthful curiosity, and it may be that I wanted to appear brave in the eyes of these men who so evidently held me more or less in contempt as a newcomer.

Blofeld accepted me, and one of the other new men offered. He was taken too.

It turned out that all the older men were married and that they were not expected to volunteer. At least there was no disgrace attaching to a refusal.

After Blofeld left, Sergeant Page told us we'd better get down to "kip" while we could. "Kip" in this case meant closing our eyes and dozing. I sat humped up in my original position through the night. There wasn't room to stretch out.

Along toward morning I began to itch, and found I had made the acquaintance of that gay and festive little soldier's enemy, the "cootie." The cootie, or the "chat" as he is called by the officers, is the common body louse. Common is right. I never got rid of mine until I left the service. Sometimes when I get to thinking about it, I believe I haven't yet.

CHAPTER III

A TRENCH RAID

In the morning the members of the raiding party were taken back a mile or so to the rear and were given instruction and rehearsal. This was the first raid that "Batt" had ever tried, and the staff was anxious to have it a success. There were fifty in the party, and Blofeld, who had organized the raid, beat our instructions into us until we knew them by heart.

The object of a raid is to get into the enemy's trenches by stealth if possible, kill as many as possible, take prisoners if practicable, do a lot of damage, and get away with a whole hide.

We got back to the front trenches just before dark. I noticed a lot of metal cylinders arranged along the parapet. They were about as big as a stovepipe and four feet long, painted brown. They were the gas containers. They were arranged about four or five to a traverse, and were connected up by tubes and were covered with sandbags. This was the poison gas ready for release over the top through tubes.

Copyright by Underwood & Underwood, N. Y.
A HEAVY HOWITZER, UNDER CAMOUFLAGE.

The time set for our stunt was eleven P.M. Eleven o'clock was "zero." The system on the Western Front, and, in fact, all fronts, is to indicate the time fixed for any event as zero. Anything before or after is spoken of as plus or minus zero.

Around five o'clock we were taken back to Mechanics trench and fed—a regular meal with plenty of everything, and all good. It looked rather like giving a condemned man a hearty meal, but grub is always acceptable to a soldier.

After that we blacked our faces. This is always done to prevent the whiteness of the skin from showing under the flare lights. Also to distinguish your own men when you get to the Boche trench.

Then we wrote letters and gave up our identification discs and were served with persuader sticks or knuckle knives, and with "Mills" bombs.

The persuader is a short, heavy bludgeon with a nail-studded head. You thump Fritz on the head with it. Very handy at close quarters. The knuckle knife is a short dagger with a heavy brass hilt that covers the hand. Also very good for close work, as you can either strike or stab with it.

We moved up to the front trenches at about half-past ten. At zero minus ten, that is, ten minutes of eleven, our artillery opened up. It was the first bombardment I had ever been under, and it seemed as though all the guns in the world were banging away. Afterwards I found that it was comparatively light, but it didn't seem so then.

The guns were hardly started when there was a sound like escaping steam. Jerry leaned over and shouted in my ear: "There goes the gas. May it finish the blighters."

Blofeld came dashing up just then, very much excited because he found we had not put on our masks, through some slip-up in the orders. We got into them quick. But as it turned out there was no need. There was a fifteen-mile wind blowing, which carried the gas away from us very rapidly. In fact it blew it across the Boche trenches so fast that it didn't bother them either.

The barrage fire kept up right up to zero, as per schedule. At thirty seconds of eleven I looked at my watch and the din was at its height. At exactly eleven it stopped short. Fritz was still sending some over, but comparatively there was silence. After the ear-splitting racket it was almost still enough to hurt.

And in that silence over the top we went.

Lanes had been cut through our wire, and we got through them quickly. The trenches were about one hundred twenty yards apart and we still had nearly one hundred to go. We dropped and started to crawl. I skinned both my knees on something, probably old wire, and both hands. I could feel the blood running into my puttees, and my rifle bothered me as I was afraid of jabbing Jerry, who was just ahead of me as first bayonet man.

They say a drowning man or a man in great danger reviews his past. I didn't. I spent those few minutes wondering when the machine-gun fire would come.

I had the same "gone" feeling in the pit of the stomach that you have when you drop fast in an elevator. The skin on my face felt tight, and I remember that I wanted to pucker my nose and pull my upper lip down over my teeth.

We got clean up to their wire before they spotted us. Their entanglements had been flattened by our barrage fire, but we had to get up to pick our way through, and they saw us.

Instantly the "Very" lights began to go up in scores, and hell broke loose. They must have turned twenty machine guns on us, or at us, but their aim evidently was high, for they only "clicked" two out of our immediate party. We had started with ten men, the other fifty being divided into three more parties farther down the line.

When the machine guns started, we charged. Jerry and I were ahead as bayonet men, with the rest of the party following with buckets of "Mills" bombs and "Stokeses."

It was pretty light, there were so many flares going up from both sides. When I jumped on the parapet, there was a whaling big Boche looking up at me with his rifle resting on the sandbags. I was almost on the point of his bayonet.

For an instant I stood with a kind of paralyzed sensation, and there flashed through my mind the instructions of the manual for such a situation, only I didn't apply those instructions to this emergency.

Instead I thought—if such a flash could be called thinking—how I, as an instructor, would have told a rookie to act, working on a dummy. I had a sort of detached feeling as though this was a silly dream.

Probably this hesitation didn't last more than a second.

Then, out of the corner of my eye, I saw Jerry lunge, and I lunged too. Why that Boche did not fire I don't know. Perhaps he did and missed. Anyhow I went down and in on him, and the bayonet went through his throat.

Jerry had done his man in and all hands piled into the trench.

Then we started to race along the traverses. We found a machine gun and put an eleven-pound high-explosive "Stokes" under it. Three or four Germans appeared, running down communication trenches, and the bombers sent a few Millses after them. Then we came to a dug-out door—in fact, several, as Fritz, like a woodchuck, always has more than one entrance to his burrow. We broke these in in jig time and looked down a thirty-foot hole on a dug-out full of graybacks. There must have been a lot of them. I could plainly see four or five faces looking up with surprised expressions.

Blofeld chucked in two or three Millses and away we went.

A little farther along we came to the entrance of a mine shaft, a kind of incline running toward our lines. Blofeld went in it a little way and flashed his light. He thought it was about forty yards long. We put several of our remaining Stokeses in that and wrecked it.

Turning the corner of the next traverse, I saw Jerry drop his rifle and unlimber his persuader on a huge German who had just rounded the corner of the "bay." He made a good job of it, getting him in the face, and must have simply caved him in, but not before he had thrown a bomb. I had broken my bayonet prying the dug-out door off and had my gun up-ended—clubbed.

Photograph from Underwood & Underwood, N. Y.

OVER THE TOP ON A RAID.

When I saw that bomb coming, I bunted at it like Ty Cobb trying to sacrifice. It was the only thing to do. I choked my bat and poked at the bomb instinctively, and by sheer good luck fouled the thing over the parapet. It exploded on the other side.

"Blimme eyes," says Jerry, "that's cool work. You saved us the wooden cross that time."

We had found two more machine guns and were planting Stokeses under them when we heard the Lewises giving the recall signal. A good gunner gets so he can play a tune on a Lewis, and the device is frequently used for signals. This time he thumped out the old one—"All policemen have big feet." Rat-a-tat-tat—tat, tat.

It didn't come any too soon.

As we scrambled over the parapet we saw a big party of Germans coming up from the second trenches. They were out of the communication trenches and were coming across lots. There must have been fifty of them, outnumbering us five or six to one.

We were out of bombs, Jerry had lost his rifle, and mine had no "ammo." Blofeld fired the last shot from his revolver and, believe me, we hooked it for home.

We had been in their trenches just three and a half minutes.

Just as we were going through their wire a bomb exploded near and got Jerry in the head. We dragged him in and also the two men that had been clicked on the first fire. Jerry got Blighty on his wound, but was back in two months. The second time he wasn't so lucky. He lies now somewhere in France with a wooden cross over his head.

Did that muddy old trench look good when we tumbled in? Oh, Boy! The staff was tickled to pieces and complimented us all. We were sent out of the lines that night and in billets got hot food, high-grade "fags", a real bath, a good stiff rum ration, and letters from home.

Next morning we heard the results of the raid. One party of twelve never returned. Besides that we lost seven men killed. The German loss was estimated at about one hundred casualties, six machine guns and several dug-outs destroyed, and one mine shaft put out of business. We also brought back documents of value found by one party in an officer's dug-out.

Blofeld got the military cross for the night's work, and several of the enlisted men got the D.C.M.

Altogether it was a successful raid. The best part of it was getting back.

CHAPTER IV

A FEW DAYS' REST IN BILLETS

After the strafing we had given Fritz on the raid, he behaved himself reasonably well for quite a while. It was the first raid that had been made on that sector for a long time, and we had no doubt caught the Germans off their guard.

Anyhow for quite a spell afterwards they were very "windy" and would send up the "Very" lights on the slightest provocation and start the "typewriters" a-rattling. Fritz was right on the job with his eye peeled all the time.

In fact he was so keen that another raid that was attempted ten days later failed completely because of a rapidly concentrated and heavy machine-gun fire, and in another, a day or two later, our men never got beyond our own wire and had thirty-eight casualties out of fifty men engaged.

But so far as anything but defensive work was concerned, Fritz was very meek. He sent over very few "minnies" or rifle grenades, and there was hardly any shelling of the sector.

Directly after the raid, we who were in the party had a couple of days "on our own" at the little village of Bully-Grenay, less than three miles behind the lines. This is directly opposite Lens, the better known town which figures so often in the dispatches.

Bully-Grenay had been a place of perhaps one thousand people. It had been fought over and through and around early in the war, and was pretty well battered up. There were a few houses left unhit and the town hall and several shops. The rest of the place was ruins, but about two hundred of the inhabitants still stuck to their old homes. For some reason the Germans did not shell Bully-Grenay, that is, not often. Once in a while they would lob one in just to let the people know they were not forgotten.

There was a suspicion that there were spies in the town and that that accounted for the Germans laying off, but whatever was the cause the place was safer than most villages so near the lines.

Those two days in repose at Bully-Grenay were a good deal of a farce. We were entirely "on our own", it is true, no parade, no duty of any kind—but the quarters—oof! We were billeted in the cellars of the battered-down houses. They weren't shell-proof. That didn't matter much, as there wasn't any shelling, but there might have been. The cellars were dangerous enough without, what with tottering walls and overhanging chunks of masonry.

Moreover they were a long way from waterproof. Imagine trying to find a place to sleep in an old ruin half full of rainwater. The dry places were piled up with brick and mortar, but we managed to clean up some half-sheltered spots for "kip" and we lived through it.

The worst feature of these billets was the rats. They were the biggest I ever saw, great, filthy, evil-smelling, grayish-red fellows, as big as a good-sized cat. They would hop out of the walls and scuttle across your face with their wet, cold feet, and it was enough to drive you insane. One chap in our party had a natural horror of rats, and he nearly went crazy. We had to "kip" with our greatcoats pulled up over our heads, and then the beggars would go down and nibble at our boots.

The first day somebody found a fox terrier, evidently lost and probably the pet of some officer. We weren't allowed to carry mascots, although we had a kitten that we smuggled along for a long time. This terrier was a well-bred little fellow, and we grabbed him. We spent a good part of both mornings digging out rats for him and staged some of the grandest fights ever.

Most of the day we spent at a little *estaminet* across the way from our so-called billets. There was a pretty mademoiselle there who served the rotten French beer and *vin blanc*, and the Tommies tried their French on her. They might as well have talked Choctaw. I speak the language a little and tried to monopolize the lady, and did, which didn't increase my popularity any.

"I say, Yank," some one would call, "don't be a blinkin' 'og. Give somebody else a chawnce."

Whereupon I would pursue my conquest all the more ardently. I was making a large hit, as I thought, when in came an officer. After that I was ignored, to the huge delight of the Tommies, who joshed me unmercifully. They discovered that my middle name was Derby, and they christened me "Darby the Yank." Darby I remained as long as I was with them.

Some of the questions the men asked about the States were certainly funny. One chap asked what language we spoke over here. I thought he was spoofing, but he actually meant it. He thought we spoke something like Italian, he said. I couldn't resist the temptation, and filled him up with a line of ghost stories about wild Indians just outside Boston. I told him I left because of a raid in which the redskins scalped people on Boston Common. After that he used to pester the life out of me for Wild West yarns with the scenes laid in New England.

One chap was amazed and, I think, a little incredulous because I didn't know a man named Fisk in Des Moines.

We went back to the trenches again and were there five days. I was out one night on barbed wire work, which is dangerous at any time, and was especially so with Fritz in his condition of jumpy nerves. You have to do most of the work lying on your back in the mud, and if you jingle the wire, Fritz traverses No Man's Land with his rapid-firers with a fair chance of bagging something.

I also had one night on patrol, which later became my favorite game. I will tell more about it in another chapter.

At the end of the five days the whole battalion was pulled out for rest. We marched a few miles to the rear and came to the village of Petite-Saens. This town had been fought through, but for some reason had suffered little. Few of the houses had been damaged, and we had real billets.

My section, ten men besides myself, drew a big attic in a clean house. There was loads of room and the roof was tight and there were no rats. It was oriental luxury after Bully-Grenay and the trenches, and for a wonder nobody had a word of "grousing" over "kipping" on the bare floor.

The house was occupied by a very old peasant woman and a very little girl, three years old, and as pretty as a picture. The old woman looked ill and sad and very lonesome. One night as we sat in her kitchen drinking black coffee and cognac, I persuaded her to tell her story. It was, on the whole, rather a cruel thing to ask, I am afraid. It is only one of many such that I heard over there. France has, indeed, suffered. I set down here, as nearly as I can translate, what the old woman said:

"Monsieur, I am very, very old now, almost eighty, but I am a patriot and I love my France. I do not complain that I have lost everything in this war. I do not care now, for I am old and it is for my country; but there is much sadness for me to remember, and it is with great bitterness that I think of the pig Allemand—beast that he is.

"Two years ago I lived in this house, happy with my daughter and her husband and the little baby, and my husband, who worked in the mines. He was too old to fight, but when the great war came he tried to enlist, but they would not listen to him, and he returned to work, that the country should not be without coal.

"The beau-fils (son-in-law), he enlisted and said good-by and went to the service.

"By and by the Boche come and in a great battle not far from this very house the beau-fils is wounded very badly and is brought to the house by comrades to die.

"The Boche come into the village, but the beau-fils is too weak to go. The Boche come into the house, seize my daughter, and there—they—oh, monsieur—the things one may not say—and we so helpless.

"Her father tries to protect her, but he is knocked down. I try, but they hold my feet over the fire until the very flesh cooks. See for yourselves the burns on my feet still.

"My husband dies from the blow he gets, for he is very old, over ninety. Just then mon beau-fils sees a revolver that hangs by the side of the German officer, and putting all his strength together he leaps forward and grabs the revolver. And there he shoots the officer—and my poor little daughter—and then he says good-by and through the head sends a bullet.

"The Germans did not touch me but once after that, and then they knocked me to the floor when they came after the pig officer. By and by come you English, and all is well for dear France once more; but I am very desolate now. I am alone but for the petite-fille (granddaughter), but I love the English, for they save my home and my dear country."

I heard a good many stories of this kind off and on, but this particular one, I think, brought home, to me at least, the general beastliness of the Hun closer than ever before. We all loved our little kiddie very much, and when we saw the evidence of the terrible cruelties the poor old woman had suffered we saw red. Most of us cried a little. I think that that one story made each of us that heard it a mean, vicious fighter for the rest of our service. I know it did me.

One of the first things a British soldier learns is to keep himself clean. He can't do it, and he's as filthy as a pig all the time he is in the trenches, but he tries. He is always shaving, even under fire, and show him running water and he goes to it like a duck.

More than once I have shaved in a periscope mirror pegged into the side of a trench, with the bullets snapping overhead, and rubbed my face with wet tea leaves afterward to freshen up.

Back in billets the very first thing that comes off is the big clean-up. Uniforms are brushed up, and equipment put in order. Then comes the bath, the most thorough possible under the conditions. After that comes the "cootie carnival", better known as the "shirt hunt." The cootie is the soldier's worst enemy. He's worse than the Hun. You can't get rid of him wherever you are, in the trenches or in billets, and he sticks closer than a brother. The cootie is a good deal of an acrobat. His policy of attack is to hang on to the shirt and to nibble at the occupant. Pull off the shirt and he comes with it. Hence the shirt hunt. Tommy gets out in the open somewhere so as not to shed his little companions indoors—there's always enough there anyhow—and he peels. Then he systematically runs down each seam—the cootie's favorite hiding place—catches the game, and ends his career by cracking him between the thumb nails.

For some obscure psychological reason, Tommy seems to like company on one of these hunts. Perhaps it is because misery loves company, or it may be that he likes to compare notes on the catch. Anyhow, it is a common thing to see from a dozen to twenty soldiers with their shirts off, hunting cooties.

"Hi sye, 'Arry," you'll hear some one sing out. "Look 'ere. Strike me bloomin' well pink but this one 'ere's got a black stripe along 'is back."

Or, "If this don't look like the one I showed ye 'fore we went into the blinkin' line. 'Ow'd 'e git loose?"

And then, as likely as not, a little farther away, behind the officers' quarters, you'll hear one say:

"I say, old chap, it's deucedly peculiar I should have so many of the beastly things after putting on the Harrisons mothaw sent in the lawst parcel."

The cootie isn't at all fastidious. He will bite the British aristocrat as soon as anybody else. He finds his way into all branches of the service, and I have even seen a dignified colonel wiggle his shoulders anxiously.

Some of the cootie stories have become classical, like this one which was told from the North Sea to the Swiss border. It might have happened at that.

A soldier was going over the top when one of his cootie friends bit him on the calf. The soldier reached down and captured the biter. Just as he stooped, a shell whizzed over where his head would have been if he had not gone after the cootie. Holding the captive between thumb and finger, he said:

"Old feller, I cawn't give yer the Victoria Cross—but I can put yer back."

And he did.

The worst thing about the cootie is that there is no remedy for him. The shirt hunt is the only effective way for the soldier to get rid of his bosom friends. The various dopes and patent preparations guaranteed as "good for cooties" are just that. They give 'em an appetite.

CHAPTER V

FEEDING THE TOMMIES

Food is a burning issue in the lives of all of us. It is the main consideration with the soldier. His life is simplified to two principal motives, *i.e.*, keeping alive himself and killing the other fellow. The question uppermost in his mind every time and all of the time, is, "When do we eat?"

In the trenches the backbone of Tommy's diet is bully beef, "Maconochie's Ration", cheese, bread or biscuit, jam, and tea. He may get some of this hot or he may eat it from the tin, all depending upon how badly Fritz is behaving.

In billets the diet is more varied. Here he gets some fresh meat, lots of bacon, and the bully and the Maconochie's come along in the form of stew. Also there is fresh bread and some dried fruit and a certain amount of sweet stuff.

It was this matter of grub that made my life a burden in the billets at Petite-Saens. I had been rather proud of being lance corporal. It was, to me, the first step along the road to being field marshal. I found, however, that a corporal is high enough to take responsibility and to get bawled out for anything that goes wrong. He's not high enough to command any consideration from those higher up, and he is so close to the men that they take out their grievances on him as a matter of course. He is neither fish, flesh, nor fowl, and his life is a burden.

I had the job of issuing the rations of our platoon, and it nearly drove me mad. Every morning I would detail a couple of men from our platoon to be standing mess orderlies for the day. They would fetch the char and bacon from the field kitchen in the morning and clean up the "dixies" after breakfast. The "dixie", by the way, is an iron box or pot, oblong in shape, capacity about four or five gallons. It fits into the field kitchen and is used for roasts, stews, char, or anything else. The cover serves to cook bacon in.

Field kitchens are drawn by horses and follow the battalion everywhere that it is safe to go, and to some places where it isn't. Two men are detailed from each company to cook, and there is usually another man who gets the sergeants' mess, besides the officers' cook, who does not as a rule use the field kitchen, but prepares the food in the house taken as the officers' mess.

As far as possible, the company cooks are men who were cooks in civil life, but not always. We drew a plumber and a navvy (road builder)—and the grub tasted of both trades. The way our company worked the kitchen problem was to have stew for two platoons one day and roast dinner for the others, and then reverse the order next day, so that we didn't have stew all the time. There were not enough "dixies" for us all to have stew the same day.

Every afternoon I would take my mess orderlies and go to the quartermaster's stores and get our allowance and carry it back to the billets in waterproof sheets. Then the stuff that was to be cooked in the kitchen went there, and the bread and that sort of material was issued direct to the men. That was where my trouble started.

The powers that were had an uncanny knack of issuing an odd number of articles to go among an even number of men, and vice versa. There would be eleven loaves of bread to go to a platoon of fifty men divided into four sections. Some of the sections would have ten men and some twelve or thirteen.

The British Tommy is a scrapper when it comes to his rations. He reminds me of an English sparrow. He's always right in there wangling for his own. He will bully and browbeat if he can, and he will coax and cajole if he can't. It would be "Hi sye, corporal. They's ten men in Number 2 section and fourteen in ourn. An' blimme if you hain't guv 'em four loaves, same as ourn. Is it right, I arsks yer? Is it?" Or,

"Lookee! Do yer call that a loaf o' bread? Looks like the A.S.C. (Army Service Corps) been using it fer a piller. Gimme another, will yer, corporal?"

When it comes to splitting seven onions nine ways, I defy any one to keep peace in the family, and every doggoned Tommy would hold out for his onion whether he liked 'em or not. Same way with a bottle of pickles to go among eleven men or a handful of raisins or apricots. Or jam or butter or anything, except bully beef or Maconochie. I never heard any one "argue the toss" on either of those commodities.

Bully is high-grade corned beef in cans and is O.K. if you like it, but it does get tiresome.

Maconochie ration is put up a pound to the can and bears a label which assures the consumer that it is a scientifically prepared, well-balanced ration. Maybe so. It is my personal opinion that the inventor brought to his task an imperfect knowledge of cookery and a perverted imagination. Open a can of Maconochie and you find a gooey gob of grease, like rancid lard. Investigate and you find chunks of carrot and other unidentifiable material, and now and then a bit of mysterious meat. The first man who ate an oyster had courage, but the last man who ate Maconochie's unheated had more. Tommy regards it as a very inferior grade of garbage. The label notwithstanding, he's right.

Many people have asked me what to send our soldiers in the line of food. I'd say stick to sweets. Cookies of any durable kind—I mean that will stand chance moisture—the sweeter the better, and if possible those containing raisins or dried fruit. Figs, dates, etc., are good. And, of course, chocolate. Personally, I never did have enough chocolate. Candy is acceptable, if it is of the sort to stand more or less rough usage which it may get before it reaches the soldier. Chewing gum is always received gladly. The army issue of sweets is limited pretty much to jam, which gets to taste all alike.

It is pathetic to see some of the messes Tommy gets together to fill his craving for dessert. The favorite is a slum composed of biscuit, water, condensed milk, raisins, and chocolate. If some of you folks at home would get one look at that concoction, let alone tasting it, you would dash out and spend your last dollar for a package to send to some lad "over there."

COOKING UNDER DIFFICULTIES.

After the excitement of dodging shells and bullets in the front trenches, life in billets seems dull. Tommy has too much time to get into mischief. It was at Petite-Saens that I first saw the Divisional Folies. This was a vaudeville show by ten men who had been actors in civil life, and who were detailed to amuse the soldiers. They charged a small admission fee and the profit went to the Red Cross.

There ought to be more recreation for the soldiers of all armies. The Y.M.C.A. is to take care of that with our boys.

By the way, we had a Y.M.C.A. hut at Petite-Saens, and I cannot say enough for this great work. No one who has not been there can know what a blessing it is to be able to go into a clean, warm, dry place and sit down to reading or games and to hear good music. Personally I am a little bit sorry that the secretaries are to be in khaki. They weren't when I left. And it sure did seem good to see a man in civilian's clothes. You get after a while so you hate the sight of a uniform.

Another thing about the Y.M.C.A. I could wish that they would have more women in the huts. Not frilly, frivolous society girls, but women from thirty-five to fifty. A soldier likes kisses as well as the next. And he takes them when he finds them. And he finds too many. But what he really wants, though, is the chance to sit down and tell his troubles to some nice, sympathetic woman who is old enough to be level-headed.

Nearly every soldier reverts more or less to a boyish point of view. He hankers for somebody to mother him. I should be glad to see many women of that type in the Y.M.C.A. work. It is one of the great needs of our army that the boys should be amused and kept clean mentally and morally. I don't believe there is any organization better qualified to do this than the Y.M.C.A.

Most of our chaps spent their time "on their own" either in the Y.M.C.A. hut or in the *estaminets* while we were in Petite-Saens. Our stop there was hardly typical of the rest in billets. Usually "rest" means that you are set to mending roads or some such fatigue duty. At Petite-Saens, however, we had it "cushy."

The routine was about like this: Up at 6:30, we fell in for three-quarters of an hour physical drill or bayonet practice. Breakfast. Inspection of ammo and gas masks. One hour drill. After that, "on our own", with nothing to do but smoke, read, and gamble.

Tommy is a great smoker. He gets a fag issue from the government, if he is lucky, of two packets or twenty a week. This lasts him with care about two days. After that he goes smokeless unless he has friends at home to send him a supply. I had friends in London who sent me about five hundred fags a week, and I was consequently popular while they lasted. This took off some of the curse of being a lance corporal.

Tommy has his favorite in "fags" like anybody else. He likes above all Wild Woodbines. This cigarette is composed of glue, cheap paper, and a poor quality of hay. Next in his affection comes Goldflakes—pretty near as bad.

People over here who have boys at the front mustn't forget the cigarette supply. Send them along early and often. There'll never be too many. Smoking is one of the soldier's few comforts. Two bits' worth of makin's a week will help one lad make life endurable. It's cheap at the price. Come through for the smoke fund whenever you get the chance.

Café life among us at Petite-Saens was mostly drinking and gambling. That is not half as bad as it sounds. The drinking was mostly confined to the slushy French beer and vin blanc and citron. Whiskey and absinthe were barred.

The gambling was on a small scale, necessarily, the British soldier not being at any time a bloated plutocrat. At the same time the games were continuous. "House" was the most popular. This is a game similar to the "lotto" we used to play as children. The backers distribute cards having fifteen numbers, forming what they call a school. Then numbered cardboard squares are drawn from a bag, the numbers being called out. When a number comes out which appears on your card, you cover it with a bit of match. If you get all your numbers covered, you call out "house", winning the pot. If there are ten people in at a franc a head, the banker holds out two francs, and the winner gets eight.

It is really quite exciting, as you may get all but one number covered and be rooting for a certain number to come. Usually when you get as close as that and sweat over a number for ten minutes, somebody else gets his first. Corporal Wells described the game as one where the winner "'ollers 'ouse and the rest 'ollers 'ell!"

Some of the nicknames for the different numbers remind one of the slang of the crap shooter. For instance, "Kelly's eye" means one. "Clickety click" is sixty-six. "Top of the house" is ninety. Other games are "crown and anchor", which is a dice game, and "pontoon", which is a card game similar to "twenty-one" or "seven and a half." Most of these are mildly discouraged by the authorities, "house" being the exception. But in any *estaminet* in a billet town you'll find one or all of them in progress all the time. The winner usually spends his winnings for beer, so the money all goes the same way, game or no game.

When there are no games on, there is usually a sing-song going. We had a merry young nuisance in our platoon named Rolfe, who had a voice like a frog and who used to insist upon singing on all occasions. Rolfie would climb on the table in the *estaminet* and sing numerous unprintable verses of his own, entitled "Oh, What a Merry Plyce is Hengland." The only redeeming feature of this song was the chorus, which everybody would roar out and which went like this:

Cheer, ye beggars, cheer!
Britannia rules the wave!
'Ard times, short times
Never'll come agyne.
Shoutin' out at th' top o' yer lungs:
Damn the German army!
Oh, wot a lovely plyce is Hengland!

Our ten days *en repos* at Petite-Saens came to an end all too soon.

On the last day we lined up for our official "bawth."

Petite-Saens was a coal-mining town. The mines were still operated, but only at night—this to avoid shelling from the Boche long-distance artillery, which are fully capable of sending shells and hitting the mark at eighteen miles. The water system of the town depended upon the pumping apparatus of the mines. Every morning early, before the pressure was off, all hands would turn out for a general "sluicing" under the hydrants. We were as clean as could be and fairly free of "cooties" at the end of a week, but official red tape demanded that we go through an authorized scouring.

On the last day we lined up for this at dawn before an old warehouse which had been fitted with crude showers. We were turned in twenty in a batch and were given four minutes to soap ourselves all over and rinse off. I was in the last lot and had just lathered up good and plenty when the water went dead. If you want to reach the acme of stickiness, try this stunt. I felt like the inside of a mucilage bottle for a week.

After the official purification we were given clean underwear. And then there was a howl. The fresh underthings had been boiled and sterilized, but the immortal cootie had come through unscathed and in all its vigor. Corporal Wells raised a pathetic wail:

"Blimme eyes, mytie! I got more'n two 'undred now an' this supposed to be a bloomin' clean shirt! Why, the blinkin' thing's as lousy as a cookoo now, an me just a-gittin' rid o' the bloomin' chats on me old un. Strike me pink if it hain't a bleedin' crime! Some one ought to write to John Bull abaht it!"

John Bull is the English paper of that name published by Horatio Bottomley, which makes a specialty of publishing complaints from soldiers and generally criticising the conduct of army affairs.

Well, we got through the bath and the next day were on our way. This time it was up the line to another sector. My one taste of trench action had made me keen for more excitement, and in spite of the comfortable time at Petite-Saens, I was glad to go. I was yet to know the real horrors and hardships of modern warfare. There were many days in those to come when I looked back upon Petite-Saens as a sort of heaven.

CHAPTER VI

HIKING TO VIMY RIDGE

We left Petite-Saens about nine o'clock Friday night and commenced our march for what we were told would be a short hike. It was pretty warm and muggy. There was a thin, low-lying mist over everything, but clear enough above, and there was a kind of poor moonlight. There was a good deal of delay in getting away, and we had begun to sweat before we started, as we were equipped as usual with about eighty pounds' weight on the back and shoulders. That eighty pounds is theoretical weight.

As a matter of practice the pack nearly always runs ten and even twenty pounds over the official equipment, as Tommy is a great little accumulator of junk. I had acquired the souvenir craze early in the game, and was toting excess baggage in the form of a Boche helmet, a mess of shell noses, and a smashed German automatic. All this ran to weight.

I carried a lot of this kind of stuff all the time I was in the service, and was constantly thinning out my collection or adding to it.

When you consider that a soldier has to carry everything he owns on his person, you'd say that he would want to fly light; but he doesn't. And that reminds me, before I forget it, I want to say something about sending boxes over there.

It is the policy of the British, and, I suppose, will be of the Americans, to move the troops about a good deal. This is done so that no one unit will become too much at home in any one line of trenches and so get careless. This moving about involves a good deal of hiking.

Now if some chap happens to get a twenty-pound box of good things just before he is shifted, he's going to be in an embarrassing position. He'll have to give it away or leave it. So—send the boxes two or three pounds at a time, and often.

But to get back to Petite-Saens. We commenced our hike as it is was getting dark. As we swung out along the once good but now badly furrowed French road, we could see the Very lights beginning to go up far off to the left, showing where the lines were. We could distinguish between our own star lights and the German by the intensity of the flare, theirs being much superior to ours, so much so that they send them up from the second-line trenches.

The sound of the guns became more distant as we swung away to the south and louder again as the road twisted back toward the front.

We began to sing the usual songs of the march and I noticed that the American ragtime was more popular among the boys than their own music. "Dixie" frequently figured in these songs.

It is always a good deal easier to march when the men sing, as it helps to keep time and puts pep into a column and makes the packs seem lighter. The officers see to it that the mouth organs get tuned up the minute a hike begins.

At the end of each hour we came to a halt for the regulation ten minutes' rest. Troops in heavy marching order move very slowly, even with the music—and the hours drag. The ten minutes' rest though goes like a flash. The men keep an eye on the watches and "wangle" for the last second.

We passed through two ruined villages with the battered walls sticking up like broken teeth and the gray moonlight shining through empty holes that had been windows. The people were gone from these places, but a dog howled over yonder. Several times we passed batteries of French artillery, and jokes and laughter came out of the half darkness.

Topping a little rise, the moon came out bright, and away ahead the silver ribbon of the Souchez gleamed for an instant; the bare poles that once had been Bouvigny Wood were behind us, and to the right, to the left, a pulverized ruin where houses had stood. Blofeld told me this was what was left of the village of Abalaine, which had been demolished some time before when the French held the sector.

At this point guides came out and met us to conduct us to the trenches. The order went down the line to fall in, single file, keeping touch, no smoking and no talking, and I supposed we were about to enter a communication trench. But no. We swung on to a "duck walk." This is a slatted wooden walk built to prevent as much as possible sinking into the mud. The ground was very soft here.

I never did know why there was no communication trench unless it was because the ground was so full of moisture. But whatever the reason, there was none, and we were right out in the open on the duck walk. The order for no talk seemed silly as we clattered along the boards, making a noise like a four-horse team on a covered bridge.

I immediately wondered whether we were near enough for the Boches to hear. I wasn't in doubt long, for they began to send over the "Berthas" in flocks. The "Bertha" is an uncommonly ugly breed of nine-inch shell loaded with H.E. It comes sailing over with a querulous "squeeeeeee", and explodes with an ear-splitting crash and a burst of murky, dull-red flame.

If it hits you fair, you disappear. At a little distance you are ripped to fragments, and a little farther off you get a case of shell-shock. Just at the edge of the destructive area the wind of the explosion whistles by your ears, and then sucks back more slowly.

The Boches had the range of that duck walk, and we began to run. Every now and then they would drop one near the walk, and from four to ten casualties would go down. There was no stopping for the wounded. They lay where they fell. We kept on the run, sometimes on the duck walk, sometimes in the mud, for three miles. I had reached the limit of my endurance when we came to a halt and rested for a little while at the foot of a slight incline. This was the "Pimple", so called on account of its rounded crest.

The Pimple forms a part of the well-known Vimy Ridge—is a semi-detached extension of it—and lies between it and the Souchez sector. After a rest here we got into the trenches skirting the Pimple and soon came out on the Quarries. This was a bowl-like depression formed by an old quarry. The place gave a natural protection and all around the edge were dug-outs which had been built by the French, running back into the hill, some of them more than a hundred feet.

In the darkness we could see braziers glowing softly red at the mouth of each burrow. There was a cheerful, mouth-watering smell of cookery on the air, a garlicky smell, with now and then a whiff of spicy wood smoke.

We were hungry and thirsty, as well as tired, and shed our packs at the dug-outs assigned us and went at the grub and the char offered us by the men we were relieving, the Northumberland Fusiliers.

The dug-outs here in the Quarries were the worst I saw in France. They were reasonably dry and roomy, but they had no ventilation except the tunnel entrance, and going back so far the air inside became simply stifling in a very short time.

I took one inhale of the interior atmosphere and decided right there that I would bivouac in the open. It was just getting down to "kip" when a sentry came up and said I would have to get inside. It seemed that Fritz had the range of the Quarries to an inch and was in the habit of sending over "minnies" at intervals just to let us know he wasn't asleep.

I had got settled down comfortably and was dozing off when there came a call for C company. I got the men from my platoon out as quickly as possible, and in half an hour we were in the trenches.

Number 10 platoon was assigned to the center sector, Number 11 to the left sector, and Number 12 to the right sector. Number 9 remained behind in supports in the Quarries.

Now when I speak of these various sectors, I mean that at this point there was no continuous line of front trenches, only isolated stretches of trench separated by intervals of from two hundred to three hundred yards of open ground. There were no dug-outs. It was impossible to leave these trenches except under cover of darkness— or to get to them or to get up rations. They were awful holes. Any raid by the Germans in large numbers at this time would have wiped us out, as there was no means of retreating or getting up reinforcements.

The Tommies called the trenches Grouse Spots. It was a good name. We got into them in the dense darkness of just before dawn. The division we relieved gave us hardly any instruction, but beat it on the hot foot, glad to get away and anxious to go before sun-up. As we settled down in our cosey danger spots I heard Rolfie, the frog-voiced baritone, humming one of his favorite coster songs:

Oh, why did I leave my little back room in old
Bloomsbury?
Where I could live for a pound a week in luxury.
I wanted to live higher
So I married Marier,
Out of the frying pan into the bloomin' fire.

And he meant every word of it.

In our new positions in the Grouse Spots the orders were to patrol the open ground between at least four times a night. That first night there was one more patrol necessary before daylight. Tired as I was, I volunteered for it. I had had one patrol before, opposite Bully-Grenay, and thought I liked the game.

I went over with one man, a fellow named Bellinger. We got out and started to crawl. All we knew was that the left sector was two hundred yards away. Machine-gun bullets were squealing and snapping overhead pretty continuously, and we had to hug the dirt. It is surprising to see how flat a man can keep and still get along at a good rate of speed. We kept straight away to the left and presently got into wire. And then we heard German voices. Ow! I went cold all over.

Then some "Very" lights went up and I saw the Boche parapet not twenty feet away. Worst of all there was a little lane through their wire at that point, and there would be, no doubt, a sap head or a listening post near. I tried to lie still and burrow into the dirt at the same time. Nothing happened. Presently the lights died, and Bellinger gave me a poke in the ribs. We started to crawfish. Why we weren't seen I don't know, but we had gone all of one hundred feet before they spotted us. Fortunately we were on the edge of a shallow shell hole when the sentry caught our movements and Fritz cut loose with the "typewriters." We rolled in. A perfect torrent of bullets ripped up the dirt and cascaded us with gravel and mud. The noise of the bullets "crackling" a yard above us was deafening.

The fusillade stopped after a bit. I was all for getting out and away immediately. Bellinger wanted to wait a while. We argued for as much as five minutes, I should think, and then the lights having gone out, I took matters in my own hands and we went away from there. Another piece of luck!

We weren't more than a minute on our way when a pair of bombs went off about over the shell hole. Evidently some bold Heinie had chucked them over to make sure of the job in case the machines hadn't. It was a close pinch—two close pinches. I was in places afterwards where there was more action and more danger, but, looking back, I don't think I was ever sicker or scareder. I would have been easy meat if they had rushed us.

We made our way back slowly, and eventually caught the gleam of steel helmets. They were British. We had stumbled upon our left sector. We found out then that the line curved and that instead of the left sector being directly to the left of ours—the center—it was to the left and to the rear. Also there was a telephone wire running from one to the other. We reported and made our way back to the center in about five minutes by feeling along the wire. That was our method afterwards, and the patrol was cushy for us.

CHAPTER VII

FASCINATION OF PATROL WORK

I want to say a word right here about patrol work in general, because for some reason it fascinated me and was my favorite game.

If you should be fortunate—or unfortunate enough, as the case might be—to be squatting in a front-line trench this fine morning and looking through a periscope, you wouldn't see much. Just over the top, not more than twenty feet away, would be your barbed-wire entanglements, a thick network of wire stretched on iron posts nearly waist high, and perhaps twelve or fifteen feet across. Then there would be an intervening stretch of from fifty to one hundred fifty yards of No Man's Land, a tortured, torn expanse of muddy soil, pitted with shell craters, and, over beyond, the German wire and his parapet.

There would be nothing alive visible. There would probably be a few corpses lying about or hanging in the wire. Everything would be still except for the flutter of some rag of a dead man's uniform. Perhaps not that. Daylight movements in No Man's Land are somehow disconcerting. Once I was in a trench where a leg—a booted German leg, stuck up stark and stiff out of the mud not twenty yards in front. Some idiotic joker on patrol hung a helmet on the foot, and all the next day that helmet dangled and swung in the breeze. It irritated the periscope watchers, and the next night it was taken down.

Ordinarily, however, there is little movement between the wires, nor behind them. And yet you know that over yonder there are thousands of men lurking in the trenches and shelters.

After dark these men, or some of them, crawl out like hunted animals and prowl in the black mystery of No Man's Land. They are the patrol.

The patrol goes out armed and equipped lightly. He has to move softly and at times very quickly. It is his duty to get as close to the enemy lines as possible and find out if they are repairing their wire or if any of their parties are out, and to get back word to the machine gunners, who immediately cut loose on the indicated spot.

Sometimes he lies with his head to the ground over some suspected area, straining his ears for the faint "scrape, scrape" that means a German mining party is down there, getting ready to plant a ton or so of high explosive, or, it may be, is preparing to touch it off at that very moment.

Always the patrol is supposed to avoid encounter with enemy patrols. He carries two or three Mills bombs and a pistol, but not for use except in extreme emergency. Also a persuader stick or a trench knife, which he may use if he is near enough to do it silently.

The patrol stares constantly through the dark and gets so he can see almost as well as a cat. He must avoid being seen. When a Very light goes up, he lies still. If he happens to be standing, he stands still. Unless the light is behind him so that he is silhouetted, he is invisible to the enemy.

Approaching a corpse, the patrol lies quiet and watches it for several minutes, unless it is one he has seen before and is acquainted with. Because sometimes the man isn't dead, but a perfectly live Boche patrol lying "doggo." You can't be too careful.

If you happen to be pussyfooting forward erect and encounter a German patrol, it is policy to scuttle back unless you are near enough to get in one good lick with the persuader. He will retreat slowly himself, and you mustn't follow him. Because: The British patrol usually goes out singly or at the most in pairs or threes.

The Germans, on the other hand, hunt in parties. One man leads. Two others follow to the rear, one to each side. And then two more, and two more, so that they form a V, like a flock of geese. Now if you follow up the lead man when he retreats, you are baited into a trap and find yourself surrounded, smothered by superior numbers, and taken prisoner. Then back to the Boche trench, where exceedingly unpleasant things are apt to happen.

It is, in fact, most unwholesome for a British patrol to be captured. I recall a case in point which I witnessed and which is far enough in the past so that it can be told. It occurred, not at Vimy Ridge, but further down the line, nearer the Somme.

I was out one night with another man, prowling in the dark, when I encountered a Canadian sergeant who was alone. There was a Canadian battalion holding the next trench to us, and another farther down. He was from the farther one. We lay in the mud and compared notes. Once, when a light floated down near us, I saw his face, and he was a man I knew, though not by name.

After a while we separated, and he went back, as he was considerably off his patrol. An hour or so later the mist began to get gray, and it was evident that dawn was near. I was a couple of hundred yards down from our battalion, and my man and I made for the trenches opposite where we were. As we climbed into a sap head, I was greeted by a Canadian corporal. He invited me to a tin of "char", and I sent my man up the line to our own position.

We sat on the fire step drinking, and I told the corporal about meeting the sergeant out in front. While we were at the "char" it kept getting lighter, and presently a pair of Lewises started to rattle a hundred yards or so away down the line. Then came a sudden commotion and a kind of low, growling shout. That is the best way I can describe it. We stood up, and below we saw men going over the top.

"What the dickens can this be?" stuttered the corporal. "There's been no barrage. There's no orders for a charge. What is it? What is it?"

Well, there they were, going over, as many as two hundred of them—growling. The corporal and I climbed out of the trench at the rear, over the parados, and ran across lots down to a point opposite where the Canadians had gone over, and watched.

They swept across No Man's Land and into the Boche trench. There was the deuce of a ruckus over there for maybe two minutes, and then back they came—carrying something. Strangely enough there had been no machine-gun fire turned on them as they crossed, nor was there as they returned. They had cleaned that German trench! And they brought back the body of a man—nailed to a rude crucifix. The thing was more like a T than a cross. It was made of planks, perhaps two by five, and the man was spiked on by his hands and feet. Across the abdomen he was riddled with bullets and again with another row a little higher up near his chest. The man was the sergeant I had talked to earlier in the night. What had happened was this. He had, no doubt, been taken by a German patrol. Probably he had refused to answer questions. Perhaps he had insulted an officer. They had crucified him and held him up above the parapet. With the first light his own comrades had naturally opened on the thing with the Lewises, not knowing what it was. When it got lighter, and they recognized the hellish thing that had been done to one of their men, they went over. Nothing in this world could have stopped them.

The M.O. who viewed the body said that without question the man had been crucified alive. Also it was said that the same thing had happened before.

I told Captain Green of the occurrence when I got back to our own trenches, and he ordered me to keep silent, which I did. It was feared that if the affair got about the men would be "windy" on patrol. However, the thing did get about and was pretty well talked over. Too many saw it.

The Canadians were reprimanded for going over without orders. But they were not punished. For their officers went with them—led them.

Occasionally the temptation is too great. Once I was out on patrol alone, having sent my man back with a message, when I encountered a Heinie. I was lying down at the time. A flock of lights went up and showed this fellow standing about ten feet from me. He had frozen and stayed that way till the flares died, but I was close enough to see that he was a German. Also—marvel of marvels—he was alone.

When the darkness settled again, I got to my feet and jumped at him. He jumped at me—another marvel. Going into the clinch I missed him with the persuader and lost my grip on it, leaving the weapon dangling by the leather loop on my wrist. He had struck at me with his automatic, which I think he must have dropped, though I'm not sure of that. Anyway we fell into each other's arms and went at it barehanded. He was bigger than I. I got under the ribs and tried to squeeze the breath out of him, but he was too rugged.

At the same time I felt that he didn't relish the clinch. I slipped my elbow up and got under his chin, forcing his head back. His breath smelled of beer and onions. I was choking him when he brought his knee up and got me in the stomach and again on the instep when he brought his heel down.

It broke my hold, and I staggered back groping for the persuader. He jumped back as far as I did. I felt somehow that he was glad. So was I. We stood for a minute, and I heard him gutter out something that sounded like "Verdamder swinehunt." Then we both backed away.

It seemed to me to be the nicest way out of the situation. No doubt he felt the same.

I seem to have wandered far from the Quarries and the Grouse Spots. Let's go back.

We were two days in the Grouse Spots and were then relieved, going back to the Quarries and taking the place of Number 9 in support. While lying there, I drew a patrol that was interesting because it was different.

The Souchez River flowed down from Abalaine and Souchez villages and through our lines to those of the Germans, and on to Lens. Spies, either in the army itself or in the villages, had been placing messages in bottles and floating them down the river to the Germans.

Somebody found this out, and a net of chicken wire had been placed across the river in No Man's Land. Some one had to go down there and fish for bottles twice nightly. I took this patrol alone. The lines were rather far apart along the river, owing to the swampy nature of the ground, which made livable trenches impossible.

I slipped out and down the slight incline, and presently found myself in a little valley. The grass was rank and high, sometimes nearly up to my chin, and the ground was slimy and treacherous. I slipped into several shell holes and was almost over my head in the stagnant, smelly water.

I made the river all right, but there was no bridge or net in sight. The river was not over ten feet wide and there was supposed to be a footbridge of two planks where the net was.

I got back into the grass and made my way downstream. Sliding gently through the grass, I kept catching my feet in something hard that felt like roots;

but there were no trees in the neighborhood. I reached down and groped in the grass and brought up a human rib. The place was full of them, and skulls. Stooping, I could see them, grinning up out of the dusk, hundreds of them. I learned afterwards that this was called the Valley of Death. Early in the war several thousand Zouaves had perished there, and no attempt had been made to bury them.

After getting out of the skeletons, I scouted along downstream and presently heard the low voices of Germans. Evidently they had found the net and planned to get the messages first. Creeping to the edge of the grass, I peeped out. I was opposite the bottle trap. I could dimly make out the forms of two men standing on the nearer end of the plank bridge. They were, I should judge, about ten yards away, and they hadn't heard me. I got out a Mills, pulled the pin, and pitched it. The bomb exploded, perhaps five feet this side of the men. One dropped, and the other ran.

After a short wait I ran over to the German. I searched him for papers, found none, and rolled him into the river.

After a few days in the Quarries we were moved to what was known as the Warren, so called because the works resembled a rabbit warren. This was on the lower side and to the left end of Vimy Ridge, and was extra dangerous. It did seem as though each place was worse than the last. The Warren was a regular network of trenches, burrows, and funk holes, and we needed them all.

The position was downhill from the Huns, and they kept sending over and down a continuous stream of "pip-squeaks", "whiz-bangs", and "minnies." The "pip-squeak" is a shell that starts with a silly "pip", goes on with a sillier "squeeeeee", and goes off with a man's-size bang.

The "whiz-bang" starts with a rough whirr like a flushing cock partridge, and goes off on contact with a tremendous bang. It is not as dangerous as it sounds, but bad enough.

The "minnie" is about the size of a two-gallon kerosene can, and comes somersaulting over in a high arc and is concentrated death and destruction when it lands. It has one virtue—you can see it coming and dodge, and at night it most considerately leaves a trail of sparks.

The Boche served us full portions of all three of these man-killers in the Warren and kept us ducking in and out pretty much all the time, night and day.

I was lucky enough after the first day to be put on sappers' duty. The Sappers, or Engineers, are the men whose duty it is to run mines under No Man's Land and plant huge quantities of explosives. There was a great amount of mining going on all the time at Vimy Ridge from both sides.

Sometimes Fritz would run a sap out reasonably near the surface, and we would counter with one lower down. Then he'd go us one better and go still deeper. Some of the mines went down and under hundreds of feet. The result of all this was that on our side at least, the Sappers were under-manned and a good many infantry were drafted into that service.

I had charge of a gang and had to fill sandbags with the earth removed from the end of the sap and get it out and pile the bags on the parapets. We were well out toward the German lines and deep under the hill when we heard them digging below us. An engineer officer came in and listened for an hour and decided that they were getting in explosives and that it was up to us to beat them to it. Digging stopped at once and we began rushing in H.E. in fifty-pound boxes. I was ordered back into supports with my section.

Right here I began to have luck. Just see how this worked out. First a rushing party was organized whose duty it was to rush the crater made by the mine explosion and occupy it before the Germans got there. Sixty men were selected, a few from each company, and placed where they were supposedly safe, but where they could get up fast. This is the most dangerous duty an infantryman has to do, because both sides after a mine explosion shower in fifty-seven varieties of sudden death, including a perfect rain of machine-gun bullets. The chances of coming out of a rushing party with a whole hide are about one in five.

Well, for a wonder, I didn't get drawn for this one, and I breathed one long, deep sigh of relief, put my hand inside my tunic and patted Dinky on the back. Dinky is my mascot. I'll tell you about him later.

On top of that another bit of luck came along, though it didn't seem like it at the moment. It was the custom for a ration party to go out each night and get up the grub. This party had to go over the duck walk and was under fire both going and coming. One of the corporals who had been out on rations two nights in succession began to "grouse."

Of course Sergeant Page spotted me and detailed me to the "wangler's" duty. I "groused" too, like a good fellow, but had to go.

"Garn," says Wellsie. "Wot's the diff if yer gets it 'ere or there. If ye clicks, I'll draw yer fags from Blighty and say a prayer for yer soul. On yer way."

Cheerful beggar, Wellsie. He was doing me a favor and didn't know it.

I did the three miles along the duck walk with the ration party, and there wasn't a shell came our way. Queer! Nor on the way back. Queerer! When we were nearly back and were about five hundred yards from the base of the Pimple, a dead silence fell on the German side of the line. There wasn't a gun nor a mortar nor even a rifle in action for a mile in either direction. There was, too, a kind of sympathetic let-up on our side. There weren't any lights going up. There was an electric tension in the very air. You could tell by the feel that something big was going to happen.

I halted the ration party at the end of the duck walk and waited. But not for long. Suddenly the "Very" lights went up from the German side, literally in hundreds, illuminating the top of the ridge and the sky behind with a thin greenish white flare. Then came a deep rumble that shook the ground, and a dull boom. A spurt of blood-red flame squirted up from the near side of the hill, and a rolling column of gray smoke.

Then another rumble, and another, and then the whole side of the ridge seemed to open up and move slowly skyward with a world-wrecking, soul-paralyzing crash. A murky red glare lit up the smoke screen, and against it a mass of tossed-up debris, and for an instant I caught the black silhouette of a whole human body spread-eagled and spinning like a pin-wheel.

Most of our party, even at the distance, were knocked down by the gigantic impact of the explosion. A shower of earth and rock chunks, some as big as a barrel, fell around us.

Then we heard a far-away cheering, and in the light of the flares we saw a newly made hill and our men swarming up it to the crater. Two mines had exploded, and the whole side of the Pimple had been torn away. Half of our rushing party were killed and we had sixty casualties from shock and wounds among men who were supposed to be at a safe distance from the mining operation. But we took and held the new crater positions.

The corporal whose place I had taken on the ration party was killed by falling stones. Inasmuch as he was where I would have been, I considered that I had had a narrow escape from "going west!" More luck!

CHAPTER VIII

ON THE GO

Marching, marching, marching,
Always ruddy well marching.
Marching all the morning,
And marching all the night.
Marching, marching, marching,
Always ruddy well marching,
Roll on till my time is up
And I shall march no more.

We sung it to the tune of "Holy, Holy, Holy", the whole blooming battalion. As we swung down the Boulevard Alsace-Lorraine in Amiens and passed the great cathedral up there to the left, on its little rise of ground, the chant lifted and lilted and throbbed up from near a thousand throats, much as the unisoned devotions of the olden monks must have done in other days.

Ours was a holy cause, but despite the association of the tune the song was far from being a holy song. It was, rather, a chanted remonstrance against all hiking and against this one in particular.

After our service at Vimy Ridge some one in authority somewhere decided that the 22nd Battalion and two others were not quite good enough for really smart work. We were, indeed, hard. But not hard enough. So some superior intellect squatting somewhere in the safety of the rear, with a finger on the pulse of the army, decreed that we were to get not only hard but tough; and to that end we were to hike. Hike we did.

For more than three weeks we went from place to place with no apparent destination, wandering aimlessly up and down the country-side of Northern France, imposing ourselves upon the people of little villages, shamming battle over their cultivated fields, and sleeping in their hen coops.

I kept a diary on that hike. It was a thing forbidden, but I managed it. One manages many things out there. I have just read over that diary. There isn't much to it but a succession of town names,—Villiers du Bois, Maisincourt, Barly, Oneaux, Canchy, Amiens, Bourdon, Villiers Bocage, Agenvilliers, Behencourt, and others that I failed to set down and have forgotten. We swept across that country, sweating under our packs, hardening our muscles, stopping here for a day, there for five days for extended-order drills and bayonet and musketry practice, and somewhere else for a sham battle. We were getting ready to go into the Somme.

The weather, by some perversity of fate, was fair during all of that hiking time. Whenever I was in the trenches it always rained, whether the season warranted it or not. Except on days when we were scheduled to go over the top. Then, probably because rain will sometimes hold up a planned-for attack, it was always fair.

On the hike, with good roads under foot, the soldier does not mind a little wet and welcomes a lot of clouds. No such luck for us. It was clear all the time. Not only clear but blazing hot August weather.

On our first march out of the Cabaret Rouge communication trench we covered a matter of ten miles to a place called Villiers du Bois. Before that I had never fully realized just what it meant to go it in full heavy equipment.

Often on the march I compared my lot with that of the medieval soldier who had done his fighting over these same fields of Northern France.

The knight of the Middle Ages was all dressed up like a hardware store with, I should judge, about a hundred pounds of armor. But he rode a horse and had a squire or some such striker trailing along in the rear with the things to make him comfortable, when the fighting was over.

The modern soldier gets very little help in his war making. He is, in fact, more likely to be helping somebody else than asking for assistance for himself. The soldier has two basic functions: first, to keep himself whole and healthy; second, to kill the other fellow. To the end that he may do these two perfectly simple things, he has to carry about eighty pounds of weight all the time.

He has a blanket, a waterproof sheet, a greatcoat, extra boots, extra underwear, a haversack with iron rations, entrenching tools, a bayonet, a water bottle, a mess kit, a rifle, two hundred fifty rounds of ammo, a tin hat, two gas helmets, and a lot of miscellaneous small junk. All this is draped, hung, and otherwise disposed over his figure by means of a web harness having more hooks than a hatrack. He parallels the old-time knight only in the matter of the steel helmet and the rifle, which, with the bayonet, corresponds to the lance, sword, and battle-ax, three in one.

The modern soldier carries all his worldly goods with him all the time. He hates to hike. But he has to.

I remember very vividly that first day. The temperature was around 90°, and some fool officers had arranged that we start at one,—the very worst time of the day. The roads so near the front were pulverized, and the dust rose in dense clouds. The long straight lines of poplars beside the road were gray with it, and the heat waves shimmered up from the fields.

Before we had gone five miles the men began to wilt. Right away I had some more of the joys of being a corporal brought home to me. I was already touched with trench fever and was away under par. That didn't make any difference.

On the march, when the men begin to weaken, an officer is sure to trot up and say:

"Corporal Holmes, just carry this man's rifle," or "Corporal Collins, take that man's pack. He's jolly well done."

Seemingly the corporal never is supposed to be jolly well done. If one complained, his officer would look at him with astounded reproach and say:

"Why, Corporal. We cawn't have this, you know! You are a Non-commissioned Officer, and you must set an example. You must, rahly."

When we finally hit the town where our billets were, we found our company quartered in an old barn. It was dirty, and there was a pigpen at one end,—very smelly in the August heat. We flopped in the ancient filth. The cooties were very active, as we were drenched with sweat and hadn't had a bath since heavens knew when. We had had about ten minutes' rest and were thinking about getting out of the harness when up came Mad Harry, one of our "leftenants", and ordered us out for foot inspection.

I don't want to say anything unfair about this man. He is dead now. I saw him die. He was brave. He knew his job all right, but he was a fine example of what an officer ought not to be. The only reason I speak of him is because I want to say something about officers in general.

This Mad Harry,—I do not give his surname for obvious reasons,—was the son of one of the richest-new-rich-merchant families in England. He was very highly educated, had, I take it, spent the most of his life with the classics. He was long and thin and sallow and fish-eyed. He spoke in a low colorless monotone, absolutely without any inflection whatever. The men thought he was balmy. Hence the nickname Mad Harry.

Mad Harry was a fiend for walking. And at the end of a twenty-mile hike in heavy marching order he would casually stroll alongside some sweating soldier and drone out,

"I say, Private Stetson. Don't you just love to hike?"

Then and there he made a lifelong personal enemy of Private Stetson. In the same or similar ways he made personal enemies of every private soldier he came in contact with.

It may do no harm to tell how Mad Harry died. He came very near being shot by one of his own men.

It was on the Somme. We were in the middle of a bit of a show, and we were all hands down in shell holes with a heavy machine-gun fire crackling overhead. I was in one hole, and in the next, which merged with mine, were two chaps who were cousins.

Mad Harry came along, walking perfectly upright, regardless of danger, with his left arm shattered. He dropped into the next shell hole and with his expressionless drawl unshaken, said, "Private X. Dress my arm."

Private X got out his own emergency bandage and fixed the arm. When it was done Mad Harry, still speaking in his monotonous drone, said:

"Now, Private X, get up out of this hole. Don't be hiding."

Private X obeyed orders without a question. He climbed out and fell with a bullet through his head. His cousin, who was a very dear friend of the boy, evidently went more or less crazy at this. I saw him leap at Mad Harry and snatch his pistol from the holster. He was, I think, about to shoot his officer when a shell burst overhead and killed them both.

Well, on this first day of the hike Mad Harry ordered us out for foot inspection, as I have said. I found that I simply couldn't get them out. They were in no condition for foot inspection,—hadn't washed for days. Harry came round and gave me a royal dressing down and ordered the whole bunch out for parade and helmet inspection. We were kept standing for an hour. You couldn't blame the men for hating an officer of that kind.

It is only fair to say that Mad Harry was not a usual type of British officer. He simply carried to excess the idea of discipline and unquestioning obedience. The principle of discipline is the guts and backbone of any army. I am inclined to think that it is more than half the making of any soldier. There has been a good deal of talk in the press about a democratic army. As a matter of fact fraternization between men and officers is impossible except in nations of exceptional temperament and imagination, like the French. The French are unique in everything. It follows that their army can do things that no other army can. It is common to see a French officer sitting in a cafe drinking with a private.

In the British army that could not be. The new British army is more democratic, no doubt, than the old. But except in the heat of battle, no British officer can relax his dignity very much. With the exception of Mr. Blofeld, who was one of those rare characters who can be personally close and sympathetic and at the same time command respect and implicit obedience, I never knew a successful officer who did not seem to be almost of another world.

Our Colonel was a fine man, but he was as dignified as a Supreme Court Judge. Incidentally he was as just. I have watched Colonel Flowers many times when he was holding orders. This is a kind of court when all men who have committed crimes and have been passed on by the captains appear before the Colonel.

Colonel Flowers would sit smiling behind his hand, and would try his hardest to find "mitigating circumstances"; but when none could be dug out he passed sentence with the last limit of severity, and the man that was up for orders didn't come again if he knew what was good for himself.

I think that on the hike we all got to know our officers better than we had known them in the trenches. Their real characters came out. You knew how far you could go with them, and what was more important, how far you couldn't go.

It was at Dieval that my rank as lance corporal was confirmed. It is customary, when a rookie has been made a non-com in training, to reduce him immediately when he gets to France. I had joined in the trenches and had volunteered for a raiding party and there had been no opportunity to reduce me. I had not, however, had a corporal's pay. My confirmation came at Dieval, and I was put on pay. I would have willingly sacrificed the pay and the so-called honor to have been a private.

Our routine throughout the hike was always about the same, that is in the intervals when we were in any one place for a day or more. It was, up at six, breakfast of tea, bread, and bacon. Drill till noon; dinner; drill till five. After that nothing to do till to-morrow, unless we got night 'ops, which was about two nights out of three.

There were few Y.M.C.A. huts so far behind the lines, and the short time up to nine was usually spent in the *estaminets*. The games of house were in full blast all the time.

On the hike we were paid weekly. Privates got five francs, corporals ten, and sergeants fifteen to twenty a week. That's a lot of money. Anything left over was held back to be paid when we got to Blighty. Parcels and mail came along with perfect regularity on that hike. It was and is a marvel to me how they do it. A battalion chasing around all over the place gets its stuff from Blighty day after day, right on the tick and without any question. I only hope that whatever the system is, our army will take advantage of it. A shortage of letters and luxury parcels is a real hardship.

We finally brought up at a place called Oneux (pronounced Oh, no) and were there five days. I fell into luck here. It was customary, when we were marching on some unsuspecting village, to send the quartermaster sergeants ahead on bicycles to locate billets. We had an old granny named Cypress, better known as Lizzie. The other sergeants were accustomed to flim-flam Lizzie to a finish on the selection of billets, with the result that C company usually slept in pigpens of stables.

The day we approached Oneux, Lizzie was sick, and I was delegated to his job. I went into the town with the three other quartermaster sergeants, got them into an *estaminet*, bought about a dollar's worth of drinks, sneaked out the back door, and preempted the schoolhouse for C company. I also took the house next door, which was big and clean, for the officers. We were royally comfortable there, and the other companies used the stables that usually fell to our lot.

As a reward, I suspect, I was picked for Orderly Corporal, a cushy job. We all of us had it fairly easy at Oneux. It was hot weather, and nights we used to sit out in the schoolhouse yard and talk about the war.

Some of the opinions voiced out there with more frankness than any one would dare to use at home would, I am sure, shock some of the patriots. The fact is that any one who has fought in France wants peace, and the sooner the better.

We had one old-timer, out since Mons, who habitually, night after night, day after day, would pipe up with the same old plaint. Something like this:

"Hi arsks yer. Wot are we fightin' for? Wot'd th' Belgiums hever do fer us? Wot? Wot'd th' Rooshians hever do fer us? Wot's th' good of th' Frenchies? Wot's th' good of hanybody but th' Henglish? Gawd lumme! I'm fed up."

And yet this man had gone out at the beginning and would fight like the very devil, and I verily believe will be homesick for the trenches if he is alive when it is all over.

Bones, who was educated and a thoughtful reader, had it figured out that the war was all due to the tyranny of the ruling classes, with the Kaiser the chief offender.

A lot of the men wanted peace at any reasonable price. Anything, so they would get back to 'Arriet or Sadie or Maria.

I should say offhand that there was not one man in a hundred who was fighting consciously for any great recognized principle. And yet, with all their grousing and criticism, and all their overwhelming desire to have it over with, every one of them was loyal and brave and a hard fighter.

A good deal has been written about the brilliancy of the Canadians and the other Colonials. Too much credit cannot be given these men. In an attack there are no troops with more dash than the Canadians, but when it comes to taking punishment and hanging on a hopeless situation, there are no troops in the wide world who can equal, much less surpass, the English. Personally I think that comparisons should be avoided. All the Allies are doing their full duty with all that is in them.

During most of the war talk, it was my habit to keep discreetly quiet. We were not in the war yet, and any remarks from me usually drew some hot shot about Mr. Wilson's "blankety-blinked bloomin' notes."

There was another American, a chap named Sanford from Virginia, in B company, and he and I used to furnish a large amount of entertainment in these war talks. Sanford was a F.F.V. and didn't care who knew it. Also he thought General Lee was the greatest military genius ever known. One night he and I got started and had it hot and heavy as to the merits of the Civil War. This for some reason tickled the Tommies half to death, and after that they would egg us on to a discussion.

One of them would slyly say, "Darby, 'oo th' blinkin' 'ell was this blighter, General Grant?"

Or, "Hi sye, Sandy, Hi 'eard Darby syin' 'ow this General Lee was a bleedin' swab."

Then Sanford and I would pass the wink and go at it tooth and nail. It was ridiculous, arguing the toss on a long-gone-by small-time scrap like the Civil War with the greatest show in history going on all around us. Anyway the Tommies loved it and would fairly howl with delight when we got to going good.

It is strange, but with so many Americans in the British service, I ran up against very few. I remember one night when we were making a night march from one village to another, we stopped for the customary ten-minutes-in-the-hour rest. Over yonder in a field there was a camp of some kind,—probably field artillery. There was dim light of a fire and the low murmur of voices. And then a fellow began to sing in a nice tenor:

Bury me not on the lone prairie
Where the wild coyotes howl o'er me.
Bury me down in the little churchyard
In a grave just six by three.

The last time I had heard that song was in New Orleans, and it was sung by a wild Texan. So I yelled, "Hello there, Texas."

He answered, "Hello, Yank. Where from?"

I answered, "Boston."

"Give my regards to Tremont Street and go to hell," says he. A gale of laughter came out of the night. Just then we had the order to fall in, and away we went. I'd like to know sometime who that chap was.

After knocking about all over the north of France seemingly, we brought up at Canchy of a Sunday afternoon. Here the whole brigade, four battalions, had church parade, and after that the band played ragtime and the officers had a gabfest and compared medals, on top of which we were soaked with two hours' steady drill. We were at Canchy ten days, and they gave it to us good and plenty. We would drill all day and after dark it would be night 'ops. Finally so many men were going to the doctor worn out that he ordered a whole day and a half of rest.

Mr. Blofeld on Saturday night suggested that, as we were going into the Somme within a few weeks, the non-coms ought to have a little blow-out. It would be the last time we would all ever be together. He furnished us with all the drinkables we could get away with, including some very choice Johnny Walker. There was a lot of canned stuff, mostly sardines. Mr. Blofeld loaned us the officers' phonograph.

It was a large, wet night. Everybody made a speech or sang a song, and we didn't go home until morning. It was a farewell party, and we went the limit. If there is one thing that the Britisher does better than another, it is getting ready to die. He does it with a smile,—and he dies with a laugh.

Poor chaps! Nearly all of them are pushing up the daisies somewhere in France. Those who are not are, with one or two exceptions, out of the army with broken bodies.

CHAPTER IX

FIRST SIGHT OF THE TANKS

Late in the summer I accumulated a nice little case of trench fever.

This disease is due to remaining for long periods in the wet and mud, to racked nerves, and, I am inclined to think, to sleeping in the foul air of the dug-outs. The chief symptom is high temperature, and the patient aches a good deal. I was sent back to a place in the neighborhood of Arras and was there a week recuperating.

While I was there a woman spy whom I had known in Abalaine was brought to the village and shot. The frequency with which the duck walk at Abalaine had been shelled, especially when ration parties or troops were going over it, had attracted a good deal of attention.

There was a single house not far from the end of that duck walk west of Abalaine, occupied by a woman and two or three children. She had lived there for years and was, so far as anybody knew, a Frenchwoman in breeding and sympathies. She was in the habit of selling coffee to the soldiers, and, of course, gossiped with them and thus gained a good deal of information about troop movements.

She was not suspected for a long time. Then a gunner of a battery which was stationed near by noticed that certain children's garments, a red shirt and a blue one and several white garments, were on the clothesline in certain arrangement on the days when troops were to be moved along the duck walk the following night. This soldier notified his officers, and evidence was accumulated that the woman was signalling to the Boche airplanes.

She was arrested, taken to the rear, and shot. I don't like to think that this woman was really French. She was, no doubt, one of the myriad of spies who were planted in France by the Germans long before the war.

After getting over the fever, I rejoined my battalion in the early part of September in the Somme district at a place called Mill Street. This was in reality a series of dug-outs along a road some little distance behind our second lines, but in the range of the German guns, which persistently tried for our artillery just beside us.

Within an hour of my arrival I was treated to a taste of one of the forms of German kultur which was new at the time. At least it was new to me—tear gas. This delectable vapor came over in shells, comparatively harmless in themselves, but which loosed a gas, smelling at first a little like pineapple. When you got a good inhale you choked, and the eyes began to run. There was no controlling the tears, and the victim would fairly drip for a long time, leaving him wholly incapacitated.

Goggles provided for this gas were nearly useless, and we all resorted to the regular gas helmet. In this way we were able to stand the stuff.

The gas mask, by the way, was the bane of my existence in the trenches—one of the banes. I found that almost invariably after I had had mine on for a few minutes I got faint. Very often I would keel over entirely. A good many of the men were affected the same way, either from the lack of air inside the mask or by the influence of the chemicals with which the protector is impregnated.

One of the closest calls I had in all my war experience was at Mills Street. And Fritz was not to blame.

Several of the men, including myself, were squatted around a brazier cooking char and getting warm, for the nights were cold, when there was a terrific explosion. Investigation proved that an unexploded bomb had been buried under the brazier, and that it had gone off as the heat penetrated the ground. It is a wonder there weren't more of these accidents, as Tommy was forever throwing away his Millses.

The Mills bomb fires by pulling out a pin which releases a lever which explodes the bomb after four seconds. Lots of men never really trust a bomb. If you have one in your pocket, you feel that the pin may somehow get out, and if it does you know that you'll go to glory in small bits. I always had that feeling myself and used to throw away my Millses and scoop a hatful of dirt over them with my foot.

This particular bomb killed one man, wounded several, and shocked all of us. Two of the men managed to "swing" a "blighty" case out of it. I could have done the same if I had been wise enough.

I think I ought to say a word right here about the psychology of the Tommy in swinging a "blighty" case.

It is the one first, last, and always ambition of the Tommy to get back to Blighty. Usually he isn't "out there" because he wants to be but because he has to be. He is a patriot all right. His love of Blighty shows that. He will fight like a bag of wildcats when he gets where the fighting is, but he isn't going around looking for trouble. He knows that his officers will find that for him a-plenty.

When he gets letters from home and knows that the wife or the "nippers" or the old mother is sick, he wants to go home. And so he puts in his time hoping for a wound that will be "cushy" enough not to discommode him much and that will be bad enough to swing Blighty on. Sometimes when he wants very much to get back he stretches his conscience to the limit—and it is pretty elastic anyhow—and he fakes all sorts of illness. The M.O. is usually a bit too clever for Tommy, however, and out and out fakes seldom get by. Sometimes they do, and in the most unexpected cases.

I had a man named Isadore Epstein in my section who was instrumental in getting Blighty for himself and one other. Issy was a tailor by trade. He was no fighting man and didn't pretend to be, and he didn't care who knew it. He was wild to get a "blighty one" or shell shock, or anything that would take him home.

One morning as we were preparing to go over the top, and the men were a little jumpy and nervous, I heard a shot behind me, and a bullet chugged into the sandbags beside my head. I whirled around, my first thought being that some one of our own men was trying to do me in. This is a thing that sometimes happens to unpopular officers and less frequently to the men. But not in this case.

It was Issy Epstein. He had been monkeying with his rifle and had shot himself in the hand. Of course, Issy was at once under suspicion of a self-inflicted wound, which is one of the worst crimes in the calendar. But the suspicion was removed instantly. Issy was hopping around, raising a terrific row.

"Oi, oi," he wailed. "I'm ruint. I'm ruint. My thimble finger is gone. My thimble finger! I'm ruint. Oi, oi, oi, oi."

The poor fellow was so sincerely desolated over the loss of his necessary finger that I couldn't accuse him of shooting himself intentionally. I detailed a man named Bealer to take Issy back to a dressing station. Well, Bealer never came back.

Months later in England I met up with Epstein and asked about Bealer. It seems that after Issy had been fixed up, the surgeon turned to Bealer and said:

"What's the matter with you?"

Bealer happened to be dreaming of something else and didn't answer.

"I say," barked the doctor, "speak up. What's wrong?"

Bealer was startled and jumped and begun to stutter.

"Oh, I see," said the surgeon. "Shell shock."

Bealer was bright enough and quick enough after that to play it up and was tagged for Blighty. He had it thrust upon him. And you can bet he grabbed it and thanked his lucky stars.

We had been on Mill Street a day and a night when an order came for our company to move up to the second line and to be ready to go over the top the next day. At first there was the usual grousing, as there seemed to be no reason why our company should be picked from the whole battalion. We soon learned that all hands were going over, and after that we felt better.

We got our equipment on and started up to the second line. It was right here that I got my first dose of real honest-to-goodness modern war. The big push had been on all summer, and the whole of the Somme district was battered and smashed.

Going up from Mill Street there were no communication trenches. We were right out in the open, exposed to rifle and machine-gun fire and to shrapnel, and the Boches were fairly raining it in on the territory they had been pushed back from and of which they had the range to an inch. We went up under that steady fire for a full hour. The casualties were heavy, and the galling part of it was that we couldn't hurry, it was so dark. Every time a shell burst overhead and the shrapnel pattered in the dirt all about, I kissed myself good-by and thought of the baked beans at home. Men kept falling, and I wished I hadn't enlisted.

When we finally got up to the trench, believe me, we didn't need any orders to get in. We relieved the Black Watch, and they encouraged us by telling us they had lost over half their men in that trench, and that Fritz kept a constant fire on it. They didn't need to tell us. The big boys were coming over all the time.

The dead here were enough to give you the horrors. I had never seen so many before and never saw so many afterwards in one place. They were all over the place, both Germans and our own men. And in all states of mutilation and decomposition.

There were arms and legs sticking out of the trench sides. You could tell their nationality by the uniforms. The Scotch predominated. And their dead lay in the trenches and outside and hanging over the edges. I think it was here that I first got the real meaning of that old quotation about the curse of a dead man's eye. With so many lying about, there were always eyes staring at you.

Sometimes a particularly wide-staring corpse would seem to follow you with his gaze, like one of these posters with the pointing finger that they use to advertise Liberty Bonds. We would cover them up or turn them over. Here and there one would have a scornful death smile on his lips, as though he were laughing at the folly of the whole thing.

The stench here was appalling. That frightful, sickening smell that strikes one in the face like something tangible. Ugh! I immediately grew dizzy and faint and had a mad desire to run. I think if I hadn't been a non-com with a certain small amount of responsibility to live up to, I should have gone crazy.

I managed to pull myself together and placed my men as comfortably as possible. The Germans were five hundred yards away, and there was but little danger of an attack, so comparatively few had to "stand to." The rest took to the shelters.

I found a little two-man shelter that everybody else had avoided and crawled in. I crowded up against a man in there and spoke to him. He didn't answer and then suddenly I became aware of a stench more powerful than ordinary. I put out my hand and thrust it into a slimy, cold mess. I had found a dead German with a gaping, putrefying wound in his abdomen. I crawled out of that shelter, gagging and retching. This time I simply couldn't smother my impulse to run, and run I did, into the next traverse, where I sank weak and faint on the fire step. I sat there the rest of the night, regardless of shells, my mind milling wildly on the problem of war and the reason thereof and cursing myself for a fool.

It was very early in the morning when Wells shook me up with, "Hi sye, Darby, wot the blinkin' blazes is that noise?"

We listened, and away from the rear came a tremendous whirring, burring, rumbling buzz, like a swarm of giant bees. I thought of everything from a Zeppelin to a donkey engine but couldn't make it out. Blofeld ran around the corner of a traverse and told us to get the men out. He didn't know what was coming and wasn't taking any chances.

It was getting a little light though heavily misty. We waited, and then out of the gray blanket of fog waddled the great steel monsters that we were to know afterwards as the "tanks." I shall never forget it.

Copyright by Underwood & Underwood, N. Y.

HEAD-ON VIEW OF A BRITISH TANK.

In the half darkness they looked twice as big as they really were. They lurched forward, slow, clumsy but irresistible, nosing down into shell holes and out, crushing the unburied dead, sliding over mere trenches as though they did not exist.

There were five in all. One passed directly over us. We scuttled out of the way, and the men let go a cheer. For we knew that here was something that could and would win battles.

The tanks were an absolutely new thing to us. Their secret had been guarded so carefully even in our own army that our battalion had heard nothing of them.

But we didn't need to be told that they would be effective. One look was enough to convince us. Later it convinced Fritzie.

CHAPTER X

FOLLOWING THE TANKS INTO BATTLE

The tanks passed beyond us and half-way up to the first line and stopped. Trapdoors in the decks opened, and the crews poured out and began to pile sandbags in front of the machines so that when day broke fully and the mists lifted, the enemy could not see what had been brought up in the night.

Day dawned, and a frisky little breeze from the west scattered the fog and swept the sky clean. There wasn't a cloud by eight o'clock. The sun shone bright, and we cursed it, for if it had been rainy the attack would not have been made.

We made the usual last preparations that morning, such as writing letters and delivering farewell messages; and the latest rooks made their wills in the little blanks provided for the purpose in the back of the pay books. We judged from the number of dead and the evident punishment other divisions had taken there that the chances of coming back would be slim. Around nine o'clock Captain Green gave us a little talk that confirmed our suspicions that the day was to be a hard one.

He said, as nearly as I can remember:

"Lads, I want to tell you that there is to be a most important battle—one of the most important in the whole war. High Wood out there commands a view of the whole of this part of the Somme and is most valuable. There are estimated to be about ten thousand Germans in that wood and in the surrounding supports. The positions are mostly of concrete with hundreds of machine guns and field artillery. Our heavies have for some reason made no impression on them, and regiment after regiment has attempted to take the woods and failed with heavy losses. Now it is up to the 47th Division to do the seemingly impossible. Zero is at eleven. We go over then. The best of luck and God bless you."

We were all feeling pretty sour on the world when the sky pilot came along and cheered us up.

He was a good little man, that chaplain, brave as they make 'em. He always went over the top with us and was in the thick of the fighting, and he had the military cross for bravery. He passed down the line, giving us a slap on the back or a hand grip and started us singing. No gospel hymns either, but any old rollicking, good-natured song that he happened to think of that would loosen things up and relieve the tension.

Somehow he made you feel that you wouldn't mind going to hell if he was along, and you knew that he'd be willing to come if he could do any good. A good little man! Peace to his ashes.

At ten o'clock things busted loose, and the most intense bombardment ever known in warfare up to that time began. Thousands of guns, both French and English, in fact every available gun within a radius of fifteen miles, poured it in. In the Bedlamitish din and roar it was impossible to hear the next man unless he put his mouth up close to your ear and yelled.

My ear drums ached, and I thought I should go insane if the racket didn't stop. I was frightfully nervous and scared, but tried not to show it. An officer or a non-com must conceal his nervousness, though he be dying with fright.

The faces of the men were hard-set and pale. Some of them looked positively green. They smoked fag after fag, lighting the new ones on the butts.

All through the bombardment Fritz was comparatively quiet. He was saving all his for the time when we should come over. Probably, too, he was holed up to a large extent in his concrete dug-outs. I looked over the top once or twice and wondered if I, too, would be lying there unburied with the rats and maggots gnawing me into an unrecognizable mass. There were moments in that hour from ten to eleven when I was distinctly sorry for myself.

The time, strangely enough, went fast—as it probably does with a condemned man in his last hour. At zero minus ten the word went down the line "Ten to go" and we got to the better positions of the trench and secured our footing on the side of the parapet to make our climb over when the signal came. Some of the men gave their bayonets a last fond rub, and I looked to my bolt action to see that it worked well. I had ten rounds in the magazine, and I didn't intend to rely too much on the bayonet. At a few seconds of eleven I looked at my wrist watch and was afflicted again with that empty feeling in the solar plexus. Then the whistles shrilled; I blew mine, and over we went.

To a disinterested spectator who was far enough up in the air to be out of range it must have been a wonderful spectacle to see those thousands of men go over, wave after wave.

The terrain was level out to the point where the little hill of High Wood rose covered with the splintered poles of what had once been a forest. This position and the supports to the left and rear of it began to fairly belch machine-gun and shell fire. If Fritz had been quiet before, he gave us all he had now.

Our battalion went over from the second trench, and we got the cream of it.

The tanks were just ahead of us and lumbered along in an imposing row. They lurched down into deep craters and out again, tipped and reeled and listed, and sometimes seemed as though they must upset; but they came up each time and went on and on. And how slow they did seem to move! Lord, I thought we should never cover that five or six hundred yards.

The tank machine guns were spitting fire over the heads of our first wave, and their Hotchkiss guns were rattling. A beautiful creeping barrage preceded us. Row after row of shells burst at just the right distance ahead, spewing gobs of smoke and flashes of flame, made thin by the bright sunlight. Half a dozen airplanes circled like dragonflies up there in the blue.

There was a tank just ahead of me. I got behind it. And marched there. Slow! God, how slow! Anyhow, it kept off the machine-gun bullets, but not, the shrapnel. It was breaking over us in clouds. I felt the stunning patter of the fragments on my tin hat, cringed under it, and wondered vaguely why it didn't do me in.

Men in the front wave were going down like tenpins. Off there diagonally to the right and forward I glimpsed a blinding burst, and as much as a whole platoon went down.

Around me men were dropping all the time—men I knew. I saw Dolbsie clawing at his throat as he reeled forward, falling. I saw Vickers double up, drop his rifle, and somersault, hanging on to his abdomen.

A hundred yards away, to the right, an officer walked backwards with an automatic pistol balanced on his finger, smiling, pulling his men along like a drum major. A shell or something hit him. He disappeared in a welter of blood and half a dozen of the front file fell with him.

I thought we must be nearly there and sneaked a look around the edge of the tank. A traversing machine gun raked the mud, throwing up handfuls, and I heard the gruff "row, row" of flattened bullets as they ricocheted off the steel armor. I ducked back, and on we went.

Slow! Slow! I found myself planning what I would do when I got to the front trenches—if we ever did. There would be a grand rumpus, and I would click a dozen or more.

And then we arrived.

I don't suppose that trip across No Man's Land behind the tanks took over five minutes, but it seemed like an hour.

At the end of it my participation in the battle of High Wood ended. No, I wasn't wounded. But when we reached the Boche front trenches a strange thing happened. There was no fight worth mentioning. The tanks stopped over the trenches and blazed away right and left with their all-around traverse.

A few Boches ran out and threw silly little bombs at the monsters. The tanks, noses in air, moved slowly on. And then the Graybacks swarmed up out of shelters and dug-outs, literally in hundreds, and held up their hands, whining "Mercy, kamarad."

We took prisoners by platoons. Blofeld grabbed me and turned over a gang of thirty to me. We searched them rapidly, cut their suspenders and belts, and I started to the rear with them. They seemed glad to go. So was I.

As we hurried back over the five hundred yards that had been No Man's Land and was now British ground, I looked back and saw the irresistible tanks smashing their way through the tree stumps of High Wood, still spitting death and destruction in three directions.

Going back we were under almost as heavy fire as we had been coming up. When we were about half-way across, shrapnel burst directly over our party and seven of the prisoners were killed and half a dozen wounded. I myself was unscratched. I stuck my hand inside my tunic and patted Dinky on the back, sent up a prayer for some more luck like that, and carried on.

After getting my prisoners back to the rear, I came up again but couldn't find my battalion. I threw in with a battalion of Australians and was with them for twenty-four hours.

When I found my chaps again, the battle of High Wood was pretty well over. Our company for some reason had suffered very few casualties, less than twenty-nine. Company B, however, had been practically wiped out, losing all but thirteen men out of two hundred. The other two companies had less than one hundred casualties. We had lost about a third of our strength. It is a living wonder to me that any of us came through.

I don't believe any of us would have if it hadn't been for the tanks.

The net result of the battle of High Wood was that our troops carried on for nearly two miles beyond the position to be taken. They had to fall back but held the wood and the heights. Three of the tanks were stalled in the farther edge of the woods—out of fuel—and remained there for three days unharmed under the fire of the German guns.

Eventually some one ventured out and got some juice into them, and they returned to our lines. The tanks had proved themselves, not only as effective fighting machines, but as destroyers of German morale.

CHAPTER XI

PRISONERS

For weeks after our first introduction to the tanks they were the chief topic of conversation in our battalion. And, notwithstanding the fact that we had seen the monsters go into action, had seen what they did and the effect they had on the Boche, the details of their building and of their mechanism remained a mystery for a long time.

For weeks about all we knew about them was what we gathered from their appearance as they reeled along, camouflaged with browns and yellows like great toads, and that they were named with quaint names like "Creme de Menthe" and "Diplodocus."

Eventually I met with a member of the crews who had manned the tanks at the battle of High Wood, and I obtained from him a description of some of his sensations. It was a thing we had all wondered about,— how the men inside felt as they went over.

My tanker was a young fellow not over twenty-five, a machine gunner, and in a little *estaminet*, over a glass of citron and soda, he told me of his first battle.

"Before we went in," he said, "I was a little bit uncertain as to how we were coming out. We had tried the old boats out and had given them every reasonable test. We knew how much they would stand in the way of shells on top and in the way of bombs or mines underneath. Still there was all the difference between rehearsal and the actual going on the stage.

"When we crawled in through the trapdoor for the first time over, the shut-up feeling got me. I'd felt it before but not that way. I got to imagining what would happen if we got stalled somewhere in the Boche lines, and they built a fire around us. That was natural, because it's hot inside a tank at the best. You mustn't smoke either. I hadn't minded that in rehearsal, but in action I was crazy for a fag.

"We went across, you remember, at eleven, and the sun was shining bright. We were parboiled before we started, and when we got going good it was like a Turkish bath. I was stripped to the waist and was dripping. Besides that, when we begun to give 'em hell, the place filled with gas, and it was stifling. The old boat pitched a good deal going into shell holes, and it was all a man could do to keep his station. I put my nose up to my loop-hole to get air, but only once. The machine-gun bullets were simply rattling on our hide. Tock, tock, tock they kept drumming. The first shell that hit us must have been head on and a direct hit. There was a terrific crash, and the old girl shook all over,—seemed to pause a little even. But no harm was done. After that we breathed easier. We hadn't been quite sure that the Boche shells wouldn't do us in.

"By the time we got to the Boche trenches, we knew he hadn't anything that could hurt us. We just sat and raked him and laughed and wished it was over, so we could get the air."

I had already seen the effect of the tanks on the Germans. The batch of prisoners who had been turned over to me seemed dazed. One who spoke English said in a quavering voice:

"Gott in Himmel, Kamarad, how could one endure? These things are not human. They are not fair."

That "fair" thing made a hit with me after going against tear gas and hearing about liquid fire and such things.

The great number of the prisoners we took at High Wood were very scared looking at first and very surly. They apparently expected to be badly treated and perhaps tortured. They were tractable enough for the most part. But they needed watching, and they got it from me, as I had heard much of the treachery of the Boche prisoners.

On the way to the rear with my bunch, I ran into a little episode which showed the foolishness of trusting a German,—particularly an officer.

I was herding my lot along when we came up with about twelve in charge of a young fellow from a Leicester regiment. He was a private, and as most of his non-commissioned officers had been put out of action, he was acting corporal. We were walking together behind the prisoners, swapping notes on the fight, when one of his stopped, and no amount of coaxing would induce him to go any farther. He was an officer, of what rank I don't know, but judging from his age probably a lieutenant.

Finally Crane—that was the Leicester chap—went up to the officer, threatened him with his bayonet, and let him know that he was due for the cold steel if he didn't get up and hike.

Whereupon Mr. Fritz pulled an automatic from under his coat—he evidently had not been carefully searched—and aimed it at Crane. Crane dove at him and grabbed his wrist, but was too late. The gun went off and tore away Crane's right cheek. He didn't go down, however, and before I could get in without danger to Crane, he polished off the officer on the spot.

The prisoners looked almost pleased. I suppose they knew the officer too well. I bandaged Crane and offered to take his prisoners in, but he insisted upon carrying on. He got very weak from loss of blood after a bit, and I had two of the Boches carry him to the nearest dressing station, where they took care of him. I have often wondered whether the poor chap "clicked" it.

Eventually I got my batch of prisoners back to headquarters and turned them over. I want to say a word right here as to the treatment of the German prisoners by the British. In spite of the verified stories of the brutality shown to the Allied prisoners by the Hun, the English and French have too much humanity to retaliate. Time and again I have seen British soldiers who were bringing in Germans stop and spend their own scanty pocket money for their captives' comfort. I have done it myself.

Almost inevitably the Boche prisoners were expecting harsh treatment. I found several who said that they had been told by their officers that they would be skinned alive if they surrendered to the English. They believed it, and you could hardly blame the poor devils for being scared.

Whenever we were taking prisoners back, we always, unless we were in too much of a hurry, took them to the nearest canteen run by the Y.M.C.A. or by one of the artillery companies, and here we would buy English or American fags. And believe me, they liked them. Any one who has smoked the tobacco issued to the German army could almost understand a soldier surrendering just to get away from it.

Usually, too, we bought bread and sweets, if we could stand the price. The Heinies would bolt the food down as though they were half starved. And it was perfectly clear from the way they went after the luxuries that they got little more than the hard necessities of army fare.

At the battle of High Wood the prisoners we took ran largely to very young fellows and to men of fifty or over. Some of the youngsters said they were only seventeen and they looked not over fifteen. Many of them had never shaved.

I think the sight of those war-worn boys, haggard and hard, already touched with cruelty and blood lust, brought home to me closer than ever before what a hellish thing war is, and how keenly Germany must be suffering, along with the rest of us.

CHAPTER XII

I BECOME A BOMBER

When I found my battalion, the battle of High Wood had pretty well quieted down. We had taken the position we went after, and the fighting was going on to the north and beyond the Wood. The Big Push progressed very rapidly as the summer drew to a close. Our men were holding one of the captured positions in the neighborhood of the Wood.

It must have been two days after we went over the top with the tanks that Captain Green had me up and told me that I was promoted. At least that was what he called it. I differed with him, but didn't say so.

The Captain said that as I had had a course in bombing, he thought he would put me in the Battalion Bombers.

I protested that the honor was too great and that I really didn't think I was good enough.

After that the Captain said that he didn't *think* I was going in the bombers. He *knew* it. I was elected!

I didn't take any joy whatever in the appointment, but orders are orders and they have to be obeyed. The bombers are called the "Suicide Club" and are well named. The mortality in this branch of the service is as great if not greater than in any other.

In spite of my feelings in the matter, I accepted the decision cheerfully—like a man being sentenced to be electrocuted—and managed to convey the impression to Captain Green that I was greatly elated and that I looked forward to future performances with large relish. After that I went back to my shelter and made a new will.

That very night I was called upon to take charge of a bombing party of twelve men. A lieutenant, Mr. May, one of the bravest men I ever knew, was to be of the party and in direct command. I was to have the selection of the men.

Captain Green had me up along with Lieutenant May early in the evening, and as nearly as I can remember these were his instructions:

"Just beyond High Wood and to the left there is a sap or small trench leading to the sunken road that lies between the towns of Albert and Bapaume. That position commands a military point that we find necessary to hold before we can make another attack.

The Germans are in the trench. They have two machine guns and will raise the devil with us unless we get them out. It will cost a good many lives if we attempt to take the position by attack, but we are under the impression that a bombing party in the night on a surprise attack will be able to take it with little loss of life. Take your twelve men out there at ten o'clock and *take that trench*! You will take only bombs with you. You and Mr. May will have revolvers. After taking the trench, consolidate it, and before morning there will be relief sent out to you. The best of luck!'"

The whole thing sounded as simple as ABC. All we had to do was go over there and take the place. The captain didn't say how many Germans there would be nor what they would be doing while we were taking their comfortable little position. Indeed he seemed to quite carelessly leave the Boche out of the reckoning. I didn't. I knew that some of us, and quite probably most of us, would never come back.

I selected my men carefully, taking only the coolest and steadiest and the best bombers. Most of them were men who had been at Dover with me. I felt like an executioner when I notified them of their selection.

At nine-thirty we were ready, stripped to the lightest of necessary equipment. Each of the men was armed with a bucket of bombs. Some carried an extra supply in satchels, so we knew there would be no shortage of Millses.

Lieutenant May took us out over the top on schedule time, and we started for the position to be taken. We walked erect but in the strictest silence for about a thousand yards. At that time the distances were great on the Somme, as the Big Push was in full swing, and the advance had been fast. Trench systems had been demolished, and in many places there were only shell holes and isolated pieces of trench defended by machine guns. The whole movement had progressed so far that the lines were far apart and broken, so much so that in many cases the fighting had come back to the open work of early in the war.

Poking along out there, I had the feeling that we were an awfully long way from the comparative safety of our main body—too far away for comfort. We were. Any doubts on the matter disappeared before morning.

At the end of the thousand yards Lieutenant May gave the signal to lie down. We lay still half an hour or so and then crawled forward. Fortunately there was no barbed wire, as all entanglements had been destroyed by the terrific bombardment that had been going on for weeks. The Germans made no attempt to repair it nor did we.

We crawled along for about ten minutes, and the Lieutenant passed the word in whispers to get ready, as we were nearly on them. Each of us got out a bomb, pulled the pin with our teeth, and waited for the signal. It was fairly still. Away off to the rear, guns were going, but they seemed a long way off. Forward, and away off to the right beyond the Wood, there was a lot of rifle and machine-gun fire, and we could see the sharp little lavender stabs of flame like electric flashes. It was light enough so that we could see dimly.

Just ahead we could hear the murmur of the Huns as they chatted in the trench. They hadn't seen us. Evidently they didn't suspect and were more or less careless.

The Lieutenant waited until the sound of voices was a little louder than before, the Boches evidently being engaged in a fireside argument of some kind, and then he jumped to his feet shouting, "Now then, my lads. All together!"

We came up all standing and let 'em go. It was about fifteen yards to Fritz, and that is easy to a good bomber, as my men all were. A yell of surprise and fright went up from the trench, and they started to run. We spread out so as to get room, gave them another round of Millses, and rushed.

The trench wasn't really a trench at all. It was the remains of a perfectly good one, but had been bashed all to pieces, and was now only five or six shell craters connected by the ruined traverses. At no point was it more than waist high and in some places only knee high. We swarmed into what was left of the trench and after the Heinies. There must have been forty of them, and it didn't take them long to find out that we were only a dozen. Then they came back at us. We got into a crooked bit of traverse that was in relatively good shape and threw up a barricade of sandbags. There was any amount of them lying about.

The Germans gave us a bomb or two and considerable rifle fire, and we beat it around the corner of the bay. Then we had it back and forth, a regular seesaw game. We would chase them back from the barricade, and then they would rush us and back we would go. After we had lost three men and Lieutenant May had got a slight wound, we got desperate and got out of the trench and rushed them for further orders. We fairly showered them as we followed them up, regardless of danger to ourselves. All this scrap through they hadn't done anything with the machine guns. One was in our end of the trench, and we found that the other was out of commission. They must have been short of small-arm ammunition and bombs, because on that last strafing they cleared out and stayed.

After the row was over we counted noses and found four dead and three slightly wounded, including Lieutenant May. I detailed two men to take the wounded and the Lieutenant back. That left four of us to consolidate the position. The Lieutenant promised to return with relief, but as it turned out he was worse than he thought, and he didn't get back.

I turned to and inspected the position. It was pretty hopeless. There really wasn't much to consolidate. The whole works was knocked about and was only fit for a temporary defence. There were about a dozen German dead, and we searched them but found nothing of value. So we strengthened our cross-trench barricade and waited for the relief. It never came.

When it began to get light, the place looked even more discouraging. There was little or no cover. We knew that unless we got some sort of concealment, the airplanes would spot us, and that we would get a shell or two. So we got out the entrenching tools and dug into the side of the best part of the shallow traverse. We finally got a slight overhang scraped out. We didn't dare go very far under for fear that it would cave. We got some sandbags up on the sides and three of us crawled into the shelter. The other man made a similar place for himself a little distance off.

The day dawned clear and bright and gave promise of being hot. Along about seven we began to get hungry. A Tommy is always hungry, whether he is in danger or not. When we took account of stock and found that none of us had brought along "iron rations", we discovered that we were all nearly starved. Killing is hungry work.

We had only ourselves to blame. We had been told repeatedly never to go anywhere without "iron rations", but Tommy is a good deal of a child and unless you show him the immediate reason for a thing he is likely to disregard instructions. I rather blamed myself in this case for not seeing that the men had their emergency food. In fact, it was my duty to see that they had. But I had overlooked it. And I hadn't brought any myself.

The "iron ration" consists of a pound of "bully beef", a small tin containing tea and sugar enough for two doses, some Oxo cubes, and a few biscuits made of reinforced concrete. They are issued for just such an emergency as we were in as we lay in our isolated dugout. The soldier is apt to get into that sort of situation almost any time, and it is folly ever to be without the ration.

Well, we didn't have ours, and we knew we wouldn't get any before night, if we did then. One thing we had too much of. That was rum. The night before a bunch of us had been out on a ration party, and we had come across a Brigade Dump. This is a station where rations are left for the various companies to come and draw their own, also ammo and other necessities. There was no one about, and we had gone through the outfit. We found two cases of rum, four gallons in a case, and we promptly filled our bottles, more than a pint each.

Tommy is always very keen on his rum. The brand used in the army is high proof and burns like fire going down, but it is warming. The regular ration as served after a cold sentry go is called a "tot." It is enough to keep the cold out and make a man wish he had another. The average Tommy will steal rum whenever he can without the danger of getting caught.

It happened that all four of us were in the looting party and had our bottles full. Also it happened that we were all normally quite temperate and hadn't touched our supply.

So we all took a nip and tightened up our belts. Then we took another and another. We lay on our backs with our heads out of the burrow, packed in like sardines and looking up at the sky. Half a dozen airplanes came out and flew over. We had had a hard night and we all dozed off, at least I did, and I guess the others did also.

Around nine we all waked up, and Bones—he was the fellow in the middle—began to complain of thirst. Then we all took another nip and wished it was water. We discussed the matter of crawling down to a muddy pool at the end of the traverse and having some out of that, but passed it up as there was a dead man lying in it. Bones, who was pretty well educated—he once asked me if I had visited Emerson's home and was astounded that I hadn't—quoted from Kipling something to the effect that,

When you come to slaughter
You'll do your work on water,
An' you'll lick the bloomin' boots of 'im that's got it.

Then Bones cursed the rum and took another nip. So did the rest of us.

There was a considerable bombardment going on all the forenoon, but few shells came anywhere near us. Some shrapnel burst over us a little way off to the right, and some of the fragments fell in the trench, but on the whole the morning was uncomfortable but not dangerous.

Around half-past ten we saw an airplane fight that was almost worth the forenoon's discomfort. A lot of them had been circling around ever since daybreak. When the fight started, two of our planes were nearly over us. Suddenly we saw three Boche planes volplaning down from away up above. They grew bigger and bigger and opened with their guns when they were nearly on top of our fellows. No hits. Then all five started circling for top position. One of the Boches started to fall and came down spinning, but righted himself not more than a thousand feet up. Our anti air-craft guns opened on him, and we could see the shells bursting with little cottony puffs all around. Some of the shrapnel struck near us. They missed him, and up he went again. Presently all five came circling lower and lower, jockeying for position and spitting away with their guns. As they all got to the lower levels, the anti air-craft guns stopped firing, fearing to get our men.

Suddenly one of the Huns burst into flames and came toppling down behind his lines, his gas tank ablaze. Almost immediately one of ours dropped, also burning and behind the Boche lines.

After that it was two to one, and the fight lasted more than ten minutes. Then down went a Hun, not afire but tumbling end over end behind our lines. I learned afterwards that this fellow was unhurt and was taken prisoner. That left it an even thing. We could see half a dozen planes rushing to attack the lone Boche. He saw them too. For he turned tail and skedaddled for home.

Bonesie began to philosophize on the cold-bloodedness of air fighting and really worked himself up into an almost optimistic frame of mind. He was right in the midst of a flowery oration on our comparative safety, "nestling on the bosom of Mother Earth", when, without any warning whatever, there came a perfect avalanche of shell all around us.

I knew perfectly well that we were caught. The shells, as near as we could see, were coming from our side. Doubtless our people thought that the trench was still manned by Germans, and they were shelling for the big noon attack. Such an attack was made, as I learned afterwards, but I never saw it.

At eleven o'clock I looked at my watch. Somehow I didn't fear death, although I felt it was near. Maybe the rum was working. I turned to Bonesie and said, "What about that safety stuff, old top?"

"Cheer, cheer, Darby," said he. "We may pull through yet."

"Don't think so," I insisted. "It's us for pushing up the daisies. Good luck if we don't meet again!"

I put my hand in and patted Dinky on the back, and sent up another little prayer for luck. Then there was a terrific shock, and everything went black.

When I came out of it, I had the sensation of struggling up out of water. I thought for an instant that I was drowning. And in effect that was almost what was happening to me. I was buried, all but one side of my face. A tremendous weight pressed down on me, and I could only breathe in little gasps.

I tried to move my legs and arms and couldn't. Then I wiggled my fingers and toes to see if any bones were broken. They wiggled all right. My right nostril and eye were full of dirt; also my mouth. I spit out the dirt and moved my head until my nose and eye were clear. I ached all over.

It was along toward sundown. Up aloft a single airplane was winging toward our lines. I remember that I wondered vaguely if he was the same fellow who had been fighting just before the world fell in on me.

I tried to sing out to the rest of the men, but the best I could do was a kind of loud gurgle. There was no answer. My head was humming, and the blood seemed to be bursting my ears. I was terribly sorry for myself and tried to pull my strength together for a big try at throwing the weight off my chest, but I was absolutely helpless. Then again I slid out of consciousness.

It was dark when I struggled up through the imaginary water again. I was still breathing in gasps, and I could feel my heart going in great thumps that hurt and seemed to shake the ground. My tongue was curled up and dry, and fever was simply burning me up. My mind was clear, and I wished that I hadn't drunk that rum. Finding I could raise my head a little, I cocked it up, squinting over my cheek bones—I was on my back—and could catch the far-off flicker of the silver-green flare lights. There was a rattle of musketry off in the direction where the Boche lines ought to be. From behind came the constant boom of big guns. I lay back and watched the stars, which were bright and uncommonly low. Then a shell burst near by,—not near enough to hurt,—but buried as I was the whole earth seemed to shake. My heart stopped beating, and I went out again.

When I came to the next time, it was still dark, and somebody was lifting me on to a stretcher. My first impression was of getting a long breath. I gulped it down, and with every grateful inhalation I felt my ribs painfully snapping back into place. Oh, Lady! Didn't I just eat that air up.

And then, having gotten filled up with the long-denied oxygen, I asked, "Where's the others?"

"Ayen't no hothers," was the brief reply.

And there weren't. Later I reconstructed the occurrences of the night from what I was told by the rescuing party.

A big shell had slammed down on us, drilling Bonesie, the man in the middle, from end to end. He was demolished. The shell was a "dud", that is, it didn't explode. If it had, there wouldn't have been anything whatever left of any of us. As it was our overhang caved in, letting sandbags and earth down on the remaining man and myself. The other man was buried clean under. He had life in him still when he was dug out but "went west" in about ten minutes.

The fourth man was found dead from shrapnel. I found, too, that the two unwounded men who had gone back with Lieutenant May had both been killed on the way in. So out of the twelve men who started on the "suicide club" stunt I was the only one left. Dinky was still inside my tunic, and I laid the luck all to him.

Back in hospital I was found to be suffering from shell shock. Also my heart was pushed out of place. There were no bones broken, though I was sore all over, and several ribs were pulled around so that it was like a knife thrust at every breath. Besides that, my nerves were shattered. I jumped a foot at the slightest noise and twitched a good deal.

At the end of a week I asked the M.O. if I would get Blighty and he said he didn't think so, not directly. He rather thought that they would keep me in hospital for a month or two and see how I came out. The officer was a Canadian and had a sense of humor and was most affable. I told him if this jamming wasn't going to get me Blighty, I wanted to go back to duty and get a real one. He laughed and tagged me for a beach resort at Ault-Onival on the northern coast of France.

I was there a week and had a bully time. The place had been a fashionable watering place before the war, and when I was there the transient population was largely wealthy Belgians. They entertained a good deal and did all they could for the pleasure of the four thousand boys who were at the camp. The Y.M.C.A. had a huge tent and spread themselves in taking care of the soldiers. There were entertainments almost every night, moving pictures, and music. The food was awfully good and the beds comfortable, and that pretty nearly spells heaven to a man down from the front.

Best of all, the bathing was fine, and it was possible to keep the cooties under control,—more or less. I went in bathing two and three times daily as the sloping shore made it just as good at low tide as at high.

I think that glorious week at the beach made the hardships of the front just left behind almost worth while. My chum, Corporal Wells, who had a quaint Cockney philosophy, used to say that he liked to have the stomach ache because it felt so good when it stopped.

On the same theory I became nearly convinced that a month in the trenches was good fun because it felt so good to get out.

At the end of the week I was better but still shaky. I started pestering the M.O. to tag me for Blighty. He wouldn't, so I sprung the same proposition on him that I had on the doctor at the base,—to send me back to duty if he couldn't send me to England. The brute took me at my word and sent me back to the battalion.

I rejoined on the Somme again just as they were going back for the second time in that most awful part of the line. Many of the old faces were gone. Some had got the wooden cross, and some had gone to Blighty.

I sure was glad when old Wellsie hopped out and grabbed me.

"Gawd lumme, Darby," he said. "Hi sye, an' me thinkin' as 'ow you was back in Blighty. An' 'ere ye are yer blinkin' old self. Or is it yer bloomin' ghost. I awsks ye. Strike me pink, Yank. I'm glad."

And he was. At that I did feel more or less ghostly. I seemed to have lost some of my confidence. I expected to "go west" on the next time in. And that's a bad way to feel out there.

CHAPTER XIII

BACK ON THE SOMME AGAIN

When I rejoined the battalion they were just going into the Somme again after a two weeks' rest. They didn't like it a bit.

"Gawd lumme," says Wellsie, "'ave we got to fight th' 'ole blinkin' war. Is it right? I awsks yer. Is it?"

It was all wrong. We had been told after High Wood that we would not have to go into action again in that part of the line but that we would have a month of rest and after that would be sent up to the Ypres sector. "Wipers" hadn't been any garden of roses early in the war, but it was paradise now compared with the Somme.

It was a sad lot of men when we swung out on the road again back to the Somme, and there was less singing than usual. That first night we remained at Mametz Wood. We figured that we would get to kip while the kipping was good. There were some old Boche dug-outs in fair condition, and we were in a fair way to get comfortable. No luck!

We were hardly down to a good sleep when C company was called to fall in without equipment, and we knew that meant fatigue of some sort. I have often admired the unknown who invented that word "fatigue" as applied in a military term. He used it as a disguise for just plain hard work. It means anything whatever in the way of duty that does not have to do directly with the manning of the trenches.

This time we clicked a burial fatigue. It was my first. I never want another. I took a party of ten men and we set out, armed with picks and shovels, and, of course, rifles and bandoliers (cloth pockets containing fifty rounds of ammo).

We hiked three miles up to High Wood and in the early morning began the job of getting some of the dead under ground. We were almost exactly in the same place from which we had gone over after the tanks. I kept expecting all the time to run across the bodies of some of our own men. It was a most unpleasant feeling.

Some cleaning up had already been done, so the place was not so bad as it had been, but it was bad enough. The advance had gone forward so far that we were practically out of shell range, and we were safe working.

The burial method was to dig a pit four feet deep and big enough to hold six men. Then we packed them in. The worst part of it was that most of the bodies were pretty far gone and in the falling away stage. It was hard to move them. I had to put on my gas mask to endure the stench and so did some of the other men. Some who had done this work before rather seemed to like it.

I would search a body for identification marks and jot down the data found on a piece of paper. When the man was buried under, I would stick a rifle up over him and tuck the record into the trap in the butt of the gun where the oil bottle is carried.

When the pioneers came up, they would remove the rifle and substitute a little wooden cross with the name painted on it. The indifference with which the men soon came to regard this burial fatigue was amazing. I remember one incident of that first morning, a thing that didn't seem at all shocking at the time, but which, looking back upon it, illustrates the matter-of-factness of the soldier's viewpoint on death.

"Hi sye, Darby," sang out one fellow. "Hi got a blighter 'ere wif only one leg. Wot'll Hi do wif 'im?"

"Put him under with only one, you blinking idiot," said I.

Presently he called out again, this time with a little note of satisfaction and triumph in his voice.

"Darby, Hi sye. I got a leg for that bleeder. Fits 'im perfect."

Well, I went over and took a look and to my horror found that the fool had stuck a German leg on the body, high boot and all. I wouldn't stand for that and had it out again. I wasn't going to send a poor fellow on his last pilgrimage with any Boche leg, and said so. Later I heard this undertaking genius of a Tommy grousing and muttering to himself.

"Cawn't please Darby," says he, "no matter wot. Fawncy the blighter'd feel better wif two legs, if one was Boche. It's a fair crime sendin' 'im hover the river wif only one."

I was sure thankful when that burial fatigue was over, and early in the forenoon we started back to rest.

Rest, did I say? Not that trip. We were hardly back to Mametz and down to breakfast when along came an order to fall in for a carrying party. All that day we carried boxes of Millses up to the dump that was by High Wood, three long miles over hard going. Being a corporal had its compensations at this game, as I had no carrying to do; but inasmuch as the bombs were moved two boxes to a man, I got my share of the hard work helping men out of holes and lending a hand when they were mired.

Millses are packed with the bombs and detonators separate in the box, and the men are very careful in the handling of them. So the moving of material of this kind is wearing.

Another line of man-killers that we had to move were "toffy apples." This quaint toy is a huge bomb, perfectly round and weighing sixty pounds, with a long rod or pipe which inserts into the mortar. Toffy apples are about the awkwardest thing imaginable to carry.

This carrying stunt went on for eight long days and nights. We worked on an average sixteen hours a day. It rained nearly all the time, and we never got dried out. The food was awful, as the advance had been so fast that it was almost impossible to get up the supplies, and the men in the front trenches had the first pick of the grub. It was also up to us to get the water up to the front. The method on this was to use the five-gallon gasoline cans. Sometimes they were washed out, oftener they weren't. Always the water tasted of gas. We got the same thing, and several times I became sick drinking the stuff.

When that eight days of carrying was over, we were so fed up that we didn't care whether we clicked or not. Maybe it was good mental preparation for what was to come, for on top of it all it turned out that we were to go over the top in another big attack.

When we got that news, I got Dinky out and scolded him. Maybe I'd better tell you all about Dinky before I go any farther. Soldiers are rather prone to superstitions. Relieved of all responsibility and with most of their thinking done for them, they revert surprisingly quick to a state of more or less savage mentality. Perhaps it would be better to call the state childlike. At any rate they accumulate a lot of fool superstitions and hang to them. The height of folly and the superlative invitation to bad luck is lighting three fags on one match. When that happens one of the three is sure to click it soon.

As one out of any group of three anywhere stands a fair chance of "getting his", fag or no fag, the thing is reasonably sure to work out according to the popular belief. Most every man has his unlucky day in the trenches. One of mine was Monday. The others were Tuesday, Wednesday, Thursday, Friday, Saturday, and Sunday.

Practically every soldier carries some kind of mascot or charm. A good many are crucifixes and religious tokens. Some are coins. Corporal Wells had a sea shell with three little black spots on it. He considered three his lucky number. Thirteen was mine. My mascot was the aforesaid and much revered Dinky. Dinky was and is a small black cat made of velvet. He's entirely flat except his head, which is becomingly round with yellow glass eyes. I carried Dinky inside my tunic always and felt safer with him there. He hangs at the head of my bed now and I feel better with him there. I realize perfectly that all this sounds like tommyrot, and that superstition may be a relic of barbarism and ignorance. Never mind! Wellsie sized the situation up one day when we were talking about this very thing.

"Maybe my shell ayen't doin' me no good," says Wells. "Maybe Dinky ayen't doin' you no good. But 'e ayen't doin' ye no 'arm. So 'ang on to 'im."

I figure that if there's anything in war that "ayen't doin' ye no 'arm", it is pretty good policy to "'ang on to it."

It was Sunday the eighth day of October that the order came to move into what was called the "O.G.I.", that is, the old German first line. You will understand that this was the line the Boches had occupied a few days before and out of which they had been driven in the Big Push. In front of this trench was Eaucort Abbaye, which had been razed with the aid of the tanks.

We had watched this battle from the rear from the slight elevation of High Wood, and it had been a wonderful sight to see other men go out over the top without having ourselves to think about. They had poured out, wave after wave, a large part of them Scotch with their kilted rumps swinging in perfect time, a smashing barrage going on ahead, and the tanks lumbering along with a kind of clumsy majesty. When they hit the objective, the tanks crawled in and made short work of it.

The infantry had hard work of it after the positions were taken, as there were numerous underground caverns and passages which had to be mopped out. This was done by dropping smoke bombs in the entrances and smoking the Boches out like bees.

When we came up, we inherited these underground shelters, and they were mighty comfortable after the kipping in the muck. There were a lot of souvenirs to be picked up, and almost everybody annexed helmets and other truck that had been left behind by the Germans.

Sometimes it was dangerous to go after souvenirs too greedily. The inventive Hun had a habit of fixing up a body with a bomb under it and a tempting wrist watch on the hand. If you started to take the watch, the bomb went off, and after that you didn't care what time it was.

I accumulated a number of very fine razors, and one of the saw-tooth bayonets the Boche pioneers use. This is a perfectly hellish weapon that slips in easily and mangles terribly when it is withdrawn. I had thought that I would have a nice collection of souvenirs to take to Blighty if I ever got leave. I got the leave all right, and shortly, but the collection stayed behind.

The dug-out that Number 10 drew was built of concrete and was big enough to accommodate the entire platoon. We were well within the Boche range and early in the day had several casualties, one of them a chap named Stransfield, a young Yorkshireman who was a very good friend of mine. Stransie was sitting on the top step cleaning his rifle and was blown to pieces by a falling shell. After that we kept to cover all day and slept all the time. We needed it after the exhausting work of the past eight days.

It was along about dark when I was awakened by a runner from headquarters, which was in a dug-out a little way up the line, with word that the platoon commanders were wanted. I happened to be in command of the platoon, as Mr. Blofeld was acting second in command of the company, Sergeant Page was away in Havre as instructor for a month, and I was next senior.

I thought that probably this was merely another detail for some fatigue, so I asked Wells if he would go. He did and in about half an hour came back with a face as long as my arm. I was sitting on the fire step cleaning my rifle and Wellsie sank dejectedly down beside me.

"Darby," he sighed hopelessly, "wot th' blinkin' 'ell do you think is up now?"

I hadn't the faintest idea and said so. I had, however, as the educated Bones used to say "a premonition of impending disaster." As a premonitor I was a success. Disaster was right.

Wellsie sighed again and spilled the news.

"We're goin' over th' bleedin' top at nine. We don't 'ave to carry no tools. We're in the first bloomin' wave."

Going without tools was supposed to be a sort of consolation for being in the first wave. The other three waves carry either picks or shovels. They consolidate the trenches after they have been taken by the first wave. That is, they turn the trench around, facing the other way, to be ready for a counter attack. It is a miserable job. The tools are heavy and awkward, and the last waves get the cream of the artillery fire, as the Boche naturally does not want to take the chance of shelling the first wave for fear of getting his own men. However, the first wave gets the machine-gun fire and gets it good. At that the first wave is the preference. I have heard hundreds of men say so. Probably the reason is that a bullet, unless it is explosive, makes a relatively clean wound, while a shell fragment may mangle fearfully.

Wells and I were talking over the infernal injustice of the situation when another runner arrived from the Sergeant Major's, ordering us up for the rum issue. I went up for the rum and left Wells to break the news about going over.

I got an extra large supply, as the Sergeant Major was good humored. It was the last rum he ever served. I got enough for the full platoon and then some, which was a lot, as the platoon was well down in numbers owing to casualties. I went among the boys with a spoon and the rum in a mess tin and served out two tots instead of the customary one. After that all hands felt a little better, but not much. They were all fagged out after the week's hard work. I don't think I ever saw a more discouraged lot getting ready to go over. For myself I didn't seem to care much, I was in such rotten condition physically. I rather hoped it would be my last time.

CHAPTER XIV

THE LAST TIME OVER THE TOP

A general cleaning of rifles started, although it was dark. Mine was already in good shape, and I leaned it against the side of the trench and went below for the rest of my equipment. While I was gone, a shell fragment undid all my work by smashing the breech.

I had seen a new short German rifle in the dug-out with a bayonet and ammo, and decided to use that. I hid all my souvenirs, planning to get them when I came out if I ever came out. I hadn't much nerve left after the bashing I had taken a fortnight before and didn't hold much hope.

Our instructions were of the briefest. It was the old story that there would probably be little resistance, if any. There would be a few machine guns to stop us, but nothing more. The situation we had to handle was this: A certain small sector had held on the attacks of the few previous days, and the line had bent back around it. All we had to do was to straighten the line. We had heard this old ghost story too often to believe a word of it.

Our place had been designated where we were to get into extended formation, and our general direction was clear. We filed out of the trench at eight-thirty, and as we passed the other platoons,—we had been to the rear,— they tossed us the familiar farewell hail, "The best o' luck, mytie."

We soon found ourselves in the old sunken road that ran in front of Eaucort Abbaye. At this point we were not under observation, as a rise in the ground would have protected us even though it had been daylight. The moon was shining brilliantly, and we knew that it would not be anything in the nature of a surprise attack. We got into extended formation and waited for the order to advance. I thought I should go crazy during that short wait. Shells had begun to burst over and around us, and I was sure the next would be mine.

Presently one burst a little behind me, and down went Captain Green and the Sergeant Major with whom he had been talking. Captain Green died a few days later at Rouen, and the Sergeant Major lost an arm. This was a hard blow right at the start, and it spelled disaster. Everything started to go wrong. Mr. Blofeld was in command, and another officer thought that he was in charge. We got conflicting orders, and there was one grand mix-up. Eventually we advanced and went straight up over the ridge. We walked slap-bang into perfectly directed fire. Torrents of machine-gun bullets crackled about us, and we went forward with our heads down, like men facing into a storm. It was a living marvel that any one could come through it.

A lot of them didn't. Mr. Blofeld, who was near me, leaped in the air, letting go a hideous yell. I ran to him, disregarding the instruction not to stop to help any one. He was struck in the abdomen with an explosive bullet and was done for. I felt terribly about Mr. Blofeld, as he had been a good friend to me. He was the finest type of officer of the new English army, the rare sort who can be democratic and yet command respect. He had talked with me often, and I knew of his family and home life. He was more like an elder brother to me than a superior officer. I left Mr. Blofeld and went on.

The hail of bullets grew even worse. They whistled and cracked and squealed, and I began to wonder why on earth I didn't get mine. Men were falling on all sides and the shrieks of those hit were the worst I had heard. The darkness made it worse, and although I had been over the top before by daylight this was the last limit of hellishness. And nothing but plain, unmixed machine-gun fire. As yet there was no artillery action to amount to anything.

Once again I put my hand inside my tunic and stroked Dinky and said to him, "For God's sake, Dink, see me through this time." I meant it too. I was actually praying,—to my mascot. I realize that this was plain, unadulterated, heathenish fetish worship, but it shows what a man reverts to in the barbaric stress of war.

By this time we were within about thirty yards of the Boche parapet and could see them standing shoulder to shoulder on the fire step, swarms of them, packed in, with the bayonets gleaming. Machine guns were emplaced and vomiting death at incredibly short intervals along the parapet. Flares were going up continuously, and it was almost as light as day.

We were terribly outnumbered, and the casualties had already been so great that I saw we were in for the worst thing we had ever known. Moreover, the next waves hadn't appeared behind us.

I was in command, as all the officers and non-coms so far as I could make out had snuffed. I signalled to halt and take cover, my idea being to wait for the other waves to catch up. The men needed no second invitation to lie low. They rolled into the shell holes and burrowed where there was no cover.

I drew a pretty decent hole myself, and a man came pitching in on top of me, screaming horribly. It was Corporal Hoskins, a close friend of mine. He had it in the stomach and clicked in a minute or two.

During the few minutes that I lay in that hole, I suffered the worst mental anguish I ever knew. Seeing so many of my closest chums go west so horribly had nearly broken me, shaky as I was when the attack started. I was dripping with sweat and frightfully nauseated. A sudden overpowering impulse seized me to get out in the open and have it over with. I was ready to die.

Sooner than I ought, for the second wave had not yet shown up, I shrilled the whistle and lifted them out. It was a hopeless charge, but I was done. I would have gone at them alone. Anything to close the act. To blazes with everything!

As I scrambled out of the shell hole, there was a blinding, ear-splitting explosion slightly to my left, and I went down. I did not lose consciousness entirely. A red-hot iron was through my right arm, and some one had hit me on the left shoulder with a sledge hammer. I felt crushed,—shattered.

My impressions of the rest of that night are, for the most part, vague and indistinct; but in spots they stand out clear and vivid. The first thing I knew definitely was when Smith bent over me, cutting the sleeve out of my tunic.

"It's a Blighty one," says Smithy. That was some consolation. I was back in the shell hole, or in another, and there were five or six other fellows piled in there too. All of them were dead except Smith and a man named Collins, who had his arm clean off, and myself. Smith dressed my wound and Collins', and said:

"We'd better get out of here before Fritz rushes us. The attack was a ruddy failure, and they'll come over and bomb us out of here."

Smith and I got out of the hole and started to crawl. It appeared that he had a bullet through the thigh, though he hadn't said anything about it before. We crawled a little way, and then the bullets were flying so thick that I got an insane desire to run and get away from them. I got to my feet and legged it. So did Smith, though how he did it with a wounded thigh I don't know.

The next thing I remember I was on a stretcher. The beastly thing swayed and pitched, and I got seasick. Then came another crash directly over head, and out I went again. When I came to, my head was as clear as a bell. A shell had burst over us and had killed one stretcher bearer. The other had disappeared. Smith was there. He and I got to our feet and put our arms around each other and staggered on. The next I knew I was in the Cough Drop dressing station, so called from the peculiar formation of the place. We had tea and rum here and a couple of fags from a sergeant major of the R.A.M.C.

After that there was a ride on a flat car on a light railway and another in an ambulance with an American driver. Snatches of conversation about Broadway and a girl in Newark floated back, and I tried to work up ambition enough to sing out and ask where the chap came from. So far I hadn't had much pain. When we landed in a regular dressing station, the M.O. gave me another going over and said,

"Blighty for you, son." I had a piece of shrapnel or something through the right upper arm, clearing the bone and making a hole about as big as a half dollar. My left shoulder was full of shrapnel fragments, and began to pain like fury. More tea. More rum. More fags. Another faint. When I woke up the next time, somebody was sticking a hypodermic needle into my chest with a shot of anti-lockjaw serum, and shortly after I was tucked away in a white enameled Red Cross train with a pretty nurse taking my temperature. I loved that nurse. She looked sort of cool and holy.

I finally brought up in General Hospital Number 12 in Rouen. I was there four days and had a real bath,—a genuine boiling out. Also had some shrapnel picked out of my anatomy. I got in fairly good shape, though still in a good deal of dull pain. It was a glad day when they put a batch of us on a train for Havre, tagged for Blighty. We went direct from the train to the hospital ship, *Carisbrook Castle*. The quarters were good,—real bunks, clean sheets, good food, careful nurses. It was some different from the crowded transport that had taken me over to France.

There were a lot of German prisoners aboard, wounded, and we swapped stories with them. It was really a lot of fun comparing notes, and they were pretty good chaps on the whole. They were as glad as we were to see land. Their troubles were over for the duration of the war.

Never shall I forget that wonderful morning when I looked out and saw again the coast of England, hazy under the mists of dawn. It looked like the promised land. And it was. It meant freedom again from battle, murder, and sudden death, from trenches and stenches, rats, cooties, and all the rest that goes to make up the worst of man-made inventions, war.

It was Friday the thirteenth. And don't let anybody dare say that date is unlucky. For it brought me back to the best thing that can gladden the eyes of a broken Tommy. Blighty! Blighty!! Blighty!!!

CHAPTER XV

BITS OF BLIGHTY

Blighty meant life,—life and happiness and physical comfort. What we had left behind over there was death and mutilation and bodily and mental suffering. Up from the depths of hell we came and reached out our hands with pathetic eagerness to the good things that Blighty had for us.

I never saw a finer sight than the faces of those boys, glowing with love, as they strained their eyes for the first sight of the homeland. Those in the bunks below, unable to move, begged those on deck to come down at the first land raise and tell them how it all looked.

A lump swelled in my throat, and I prayed that I might never go back to the trenches. And I prayed, too, that the brave boys still over there might soon be out of it.

We steamed into the harbor of Southampton early in the afternoon. Within an hour all of those that could walk had gone ashore. As we got into the waiting trains the civilian populace cheered. I, like everybody else I suppose, had dreamed often of coming back sometime as a hero and being greeted as a hero. But the cheering, though it came straight from the hearts of a grateful people, seemed, after all, rather hollow. I wanted to get somewhere and rest.

It seemed good to look out of the windows and see the signs printed in English. That made it all seem less like a dream.

I was taken first to the Clearing Hospital at Eastleigh. As we got off the train there the people cheered again, and among the civilians were many wounded men who had just recently come back. They knew how we felt.

CORPORAL HOLMES WITH STAFF NURSE AND ANOTHER PATIENT,
AT FULHAM MILITARY HOSPITAL, LONDON, S.W.

The first thing at the hospital was a real honest-to-God bath. *In a tub. With hot water!* Heavens, how I wallowed. The orderly helped me and had to drag me out. I'd have stayed in that tub all night if he would have let me.

Out of the tub I had clean things straight through, with a neat blue uniform, and for once was free of the cooties. The old uniform, blood-stained and ragged, went to the baking and disinfecting plant.

That night all of us newly arrived men who could went to the Y.M.C.A. to a concert given in our honor. The chaplain came around and cheered us up and gave us good fags.

Next morning I went around to the M.O. He looked my arm over and calmly said that it would have to come off as gangrene had set in. For a moment I wished that piece of shrapnel had gone through my head. I pictured myself going around with only one arm, and the prospect didn't look good.

However, the doctor dressed the arm with the greatest care and told me I could go to a London hospital as I had asked, for I wanted to be near my people at Southall. These were the friends I had made before leaving Blighty and who had sent me weekly parcels and letters.

I arrived in London on Tuesday and was taken in a big Red Cross motor loaned by Sir Charles Dickerson to the Fulham Hospital in Hammersmith. I was overjoyed, as the hospital was very near Southall, and Mr. and Mrs. Puttee were both there to meet me.

The Sister in charge of my ward, Miss Malin, is one of the finest women I have met. I owe it to her care and skill that I still have my good right arm. She has since married and the lucky man has one of the best of wives. Miss Malin advised me right at the beginning not to submit to an amputation.

My next few weeks were pretty awful. I was in constant pain, and after the old arm began to come around under Miss Malin's treatment one of the doctors discovered that my left hand was queer. It had been somewhat swollen, but not really bad. The doctor insisted upon an X-ray and found a bit of shrapnel imbedded. He was all for an operation. Operations seemed to be the long suit of most of those doctors. I imagine they couldn't resist the temptation to get some practice with so much cheap material all about. I consented this time, and went down for the pictures on Lord Mayor's Day. Going to the pictures is Tommy's expression for undergoing an anesthetic.

I was under ether two hours and a half, and when I came out of it the left hand was all to the bad and has been ever since. There followed weeks of agonizing massage treatments. Between treatments though, I had it cushy.

My friends were very good to me, and several Americans entertained me a good deal. I had a permanent walking-out pass good from nine in the morning until nine at night. I saw almost every show in the city, and heard a special performance of the Messiah at Westminster Abbey. Also I enjoyed a good deal of restaurant life.

London is good to the wounded men. There is entertainment for all of them. A good many of these slightly wounded complain because they cannot get anything to drink, but undoubtedly it is the best thing for them. It is against the law to serve men in the blue uniform of the wounded. Men in khaki can buy all the liquor they want, the public houses being open from noon to two-thirty and from six P.M. to nine-thirty. Treating is not allowed. Altogether it works out very well and there is little drunkenness among the soldiers.

I eventually brought up in a Convalescent Hospital in Brentford, Middlesex, and was there for three weeks. At the end of that time I was placed in category C 3.

The system of marking the men in England is by categories, A, B, and C. A 1, 2, and 3 are for active service. A 4 is for the under-aged. B categories are for base service, and C is for home service. C 3 was for clerical duty, and as I was not likely to become efficient again as a soldier, it looked like some kind of bookkeeping for me for the duration of the war.

Unless one is all shot to pieces, literally with something gone, it is hard to get a discharge from the British army. Back in the early days of 1915, a leg off was about the only thing that would produce a discharge.

When I was put at clerical duty, I immediately began to furnish trouble for the British army, not intentionally, of course, but quite effectively. The first thing I did was to drop a typewriter and smash it. My hands had spells when they absolutely refused to work. Usually it was when I had something breakable in them. After I had done about two hundred dollars' damage indoors they tried me out as bayonet instructor. I immediately dropped a rifle on a concrete walk and smashed it. They wanted me to pay for it, but the M.O. called attention to the fact that I shouldn't have been put at the work under my category.

CORPORAL HOLMES WITH COMPANY OFFICE FORCE, AT WINCHESTER, ENGLAND,
A WEEK PRIOR TO DISCHARGE.

They then put me back at bookkeeping at Command Headquarters, Salisbury, but I couldn't figure English money and had a bad habit of fainting and falling off the high stool. To cap the climax, I finally fell one day and knocked down the stovepipe, and nearly set the office afire. The M.O. then ordered me back to the depot at Winchester and recommended me for discharge. I guess he thought it would be the cheapest in the long run.

The adjutant at Winchester didn't seem any too pleased to see me. He said I looked as healthy as a wolf, which I did, and that they would never let me out of the army. He seemed to think that my quite normal appearance would be looked upon as a personal insult by the medical board. I said that I was sorry I didn't have a leg or two gone, but it couldn't be helped.

While waiting for the Board, I was sent to the German Prison Camp at Winnal Downs as corporal of the permanent guard. I began to fear that at last they had found something that I could do without damaging anything, and my visions of the U.S.A. went a-glimmering. I was with the Fritzies for over a week, and they certainly have it soft and cushy.

They have as good food as the Tommies. They are paid ninepence a day, and the work they do is a joke. They are well housed and kept clean and have their own canteens, where they can buy almost anything in the way of delicacies. They are decently treated by the English soldiers, who even buy them fags out of their own money. The nearest thing I ever saw to humiliation of a German was a few good-natured jokes at their expense by some of the wits in the guard. The English know how to play fair with an enemy when they have him down.

I had about given up hope of ever getting out of the army when I was summoned to appear before the

Travelling Medical Board. You can wager I lost no time in appearing.

The board looked me over with a discouraging and cynical suspicion. I certainly did look as rugged as a navvy. When they gave me a going over, they found that my heart was out of place and that my left hand might never limber up again. They voted for a discharge in jig time. I had all I could do to keep from howling with joy.

It was some weeks before the final formalities were closed up. The pension board passed on my case, and I was given the magnificent sum of sixteen shillings and sixpence a week, or $3.75. I spent the next few weeks in visiting my friends and, eventually, at the 22nd Headquarters at Bermondsey, London, S.C., received the papers that once more made me a free man.

The papers read in part, "He is discharged in consequence of paragraph 392, King's Rules and Regulations. No longer fit for service." In another part of the book you will find a reproduction of the character discharge also given. The discharged man also receives a little silver badge bearing the inscription, "For King and Empire, Services Rendered." I think that I value this badge more than any other possession.

Once free, I lost no time in getting my passport into shape and engaged a passage on the *St. Paul*, to sail on the second of June. Since my discharge is dated the twenty-eighth of May, you can see that I didn't waste any time. My friends at Southall thought I was doing things in a good deal of a hurry. The fact is, I was fed up on war. I had had a plenty. And I was going to make my get-away before the British War Office changed its mind and got me back in uniform. Mrs. Puttee and her eldest son saw me off at Euston Station. Leaving them was the one wrench, as they had become very dear to me. But I had to go. If Blighty had looked good, the thought of the U.S.A. was better.

My passage was uneventful. No submarines, no bad weather, nothing disagreeable. On the eighth day I looked out through a welter of fog and rain to the place where the Statue of Liberty should have been waving a greeting across New York harbor. The lady wasn't visible, but I knew she was there. And even in a downpour equal to anything furnished by the choicest of Flanders rainstorms, little old New York looked better than anything I could imagine, except sober and staid old Boston.

That I am at home, safe and free of the horrors of war, is to me a strange thing. I think it comes into the experience of most of the men who have been over there and who have been invalided out of the service. Looking back on the awfulness of the trenches and the agonies of mind and body, the sacrifice seems to fade into insignificance beside the satisfaction of having done a bit in the great and just cause.

Now that our own men are going over, I find myself with a very deep regret that I cannot go too. I can only wish them the best of luck and rest in confidence that every man will do his uttermost.

CHAPTER XVI

SUGGESTIONS FOR "SAMMY"

I cannot end this book without saying something to those who have boys over there and, what is more to the point, to those boys who may go over there.

First as to the things that should be sent in parcels; and a great deal of consideration should be given to this. You must be very careful not to send things that will load your Sammy down, as every ounce counts in the pack when he is hiking, and he is likely to be hiking any time or all the time.

In the line of eatables the soldier wants something sweet. Good hard cookies are all right. I wish more people in this country knew how to make the English plum pudding in bags, the kind that will keep forever and be good when it is boiled. Mainly, though, chocolate is the thing. The milk kind is well enough, but it is apt to cause overmuch thirst. Personally I would rather have the plain chocolate,—the water variety.

Chewing gum is always in demand and is not bulky in the package. Send a lot of it. Lime and lemon tablets in the summertime are great for checking thirst on the march. A few of them won't do any harm in any parcel, summer or winter.

Now about smoking materials. Unless the man to whom the parcel is to be sent is definitely known to be prejudiced against cigarettes, don't send him pipe tobacco or a pipe. There are smokers who hate cigarettes just as there are some people who think that the little paper roll is an invention of the devil. If any one has a boy over there, he—or she—had better overcome any possible personal feeling against the use of cigarettes and send them in preference to anything else.

From my own experience I know that cigarettes are the most important thing that can be sent to a soldier. When I went out there, I was a pipe smoker. After I had been in the trenches a week I quit the pipe and threw it away. It is seldom enough that one has the opportunity to enjoy a full pipe. It is very hard to get lighted when the matches are wet in bad weather, which is nearly always. Besides which, say what you will, a pipe does not soothe the nerves as a fag does.

Now when sending the cigarettes out, don't try to think of the special brand that Harold or Percival used when he was home. Likely enough his name has changed, and instead of being Percy or Harold he is now

Pigeye or Sour-belly; and his taste in the weed has changed too. He won't be so keen on his own particular brand of Turkish. Just send him the common or garden Virginia sort at five cents the package. That is the kind that gives most comfort to the outworn Tommy or Sammy.

Don't think that you can send too many. I have had five hundred sent to me in a week many times and have none left at the end. There are always men who do not get any parcels, and they have to be looked out for. Out there all things are common property, and the soldier shares his last with his less fortunate comrade. Subscribe when you get the chance to any and all smoke funds.

Don't listen to the pestilential fuddy-duds who do not approve of tobacco, particularly the fussy-old-maids. Personally, when I hear any of these conscientious objectors to My Lady Nicotine air their opinions, I wish that they could be placed in the trenches for a while. They would soon change their minds about rum issues and tobacco, and I'll wager they would be first in the line when the issues came around.

One thing that many people forget to put in the soldier's parcel, or don't see the point of, is talcum powder. Razors get dull very quickly, and the face gets sore. The powder is almost a necessity when one is shaving in luke-warm tea and laundry soap, with a safety razor blade that wasn't sharp in the first place. In the summer on the march men sweat and accumulate all the dirt there is in the world. There are forty hitherto unsuspected places on the body that chafe under the weight of equipment. Talc helps. In the matter of sore feet, it is a life saver.

Soap,—don't forget that. Always some good, pure, plain white soap, like Ivory or Castile; and a small bath towel now and then. There is so little chance to wash towels that they soon get unusable.

In the way of wearing apparel, socks are always good. But, girlie, make 'em right. That last pair sent me nearly cost me a court martial by my getting my feet into trench-foot condition. If you can't leave out the seams, wear them yourself for a while, and see how you like it.

Sleeveless sweaters are good and easy to make, I am told. They don't last long at the best, so should not be elaborate. Any garment worn close to the body gets cooty in a few weeks and has to be ditched. However, keep right on with the knitting, with the exception of the socks. If you're not an expert on those, better buy them.

You may in that way retain the affection of your sweetheart over there.

Knitted helmets are a great comfort. I had one that was fine not only to wear under the tin hat but to sleep in. I am not keen on wristlets or gloves. Better buy the gloves you send in the shops. So that's the knitted stuff,—helmets, sweaters, and mufflers and, for the expert, socks.

Be very moderate in the matter of reading matter. I mean by that, don't send a lot at a time or any very bulky stuff at all.

If it is possible to get a louse pomade called Harrison's in this country, send it, as it is a cooty killer. So far as I know, it is the only thing sold that will do the cooty in. There's a fortune waiting for the one who compounds a louse eradicator that will kill the cooty and not irritate or nearly kill the one who uses it. I shall expect a royalty from the successful chemist who produces the much needed compound.

For the wealthier people, I would suggest that good things to send are silk shirts and drawers. It is possible to get the cooties out of these garments much easier than out of the thick woollies. There are many other things that may be sent, but I have mentioned the most important. The main thing to remember is not to run to bulk. And don't forget that it takes a long time for stuff to get across.

Don't overlook the letters,—this especially if you are a mother, wife, or sweetheart. It is an easy thing to forget. You mustn't. Out there life is chiefly squalor, filth, and stench. The boy gets disgusted and lonesome and homesick, even though he may write to the contrary. Write to him at least three times a week. Always write cheerfully, even although something may have happened that has plunged you into the depths of despair. If it is necessary to cover up something that would cause a soldier worry, cover it up. Even lie to him. It will be justified. Keep in mind the now famous, war song, "Pack up your troubles in your old kit bag and smile, smile, smile." Keep your own packed up and don't send any over there for some soldier to worry over.

Just a few words to the men themselves who may go. Don't take elaborate shaving tackle, just brush, razor, soap, and a small mirror. Most of the time you won't need the mirror. You'll use the periscope mirror in the trenches. Don't load up on books and unnecessary clothing. Impress it upon your relatives that your stuff, tobacco and sweets, is to come along in small parcels and often and regularly. Let all your friends and relatives know your address and ask them to write often. Don't hesitate to tell them all that a parcel now and again will be acceptable. Have more than one source of supply if possible.

When you get out there, hunt up the Y.M.C.A. huts. You will find good cheer, warmth, music, and above all a place to do your writing. Write home often. Your people are concerned about you all the time. Write at least once a week to the one nearest and dearest to you. I used to average ten letters a week to friends in Blighty and back here, and that was a lot more than I was allowed. I found a way. Most of you won't be able to go over your allowance. But do go the limit.

Over there you will find a lot of attractive girls and women. Most any girl is attractive when you are just out of the misery of the trenches. Be careful of them. Remember the country has been full of soldiers for three years. Don't make love too easily. One of the singers in the Divisional Follies recently revived the once popular music-hall song, "If You Can't Be Good Be Careful." It should appeal to the soldier as much as "Smile, smile, smile", and is equally good advice. For the sake of those at home and for the sake of your own peace of mind come back from overseas clean.

After all it is possible to no more than give hints to the boys who are going. All of you will have to learn by experience. My parting word to you all is just, "The best of luck."

GLOSSARY OF ARMY SLANG

All around traverse—A machine gun placed on a swivel to turn in any direction.

Ammo—Ammunition. Usually for rifles, though occasionally used to indicate that for artillery.

Argue the toss—Argue the point.

Back of the line—Anywhere to the rear and out of the danger zone.

Barbed wire—Ordinary barbed wire used for entanglements. A thicker and heavier military wire is sometimes used.

Barrage—Shells dropped simultaneously and in a row so as to form a curtain of fire. Literal translation "a barrier."

Bashed—Smashed.

Big boys—Big guns or the shells they send over.

Big push—The battles of the Somme.

Billets—The quarters of the soldier when back of the line. Any place from a pigpen to a palace.

Bleeder or Blighter—Cockney slang for fellow. Roughly corresponding to American "guy."

Blighty—England. East Indian derivation. The paradise looked forward to by all good soldiers,—and all bad ones too.

Blighty one—A wound that will take the soldier to Blighty.

Bloody—The universal Cockney adjective. It is vaguely supposed to be highly obscene, though just why nobody seems to know.

Blooming—A meaningless and greatly used adjective. Applied to anything and everything.

Bomb—A hand grenade.

Bully beef—Corned beef, high grade and good of the kind, if you like the kind. It sets hard on the chest.

Carry on—To go ahead with the matter in hand.

Char—Tea. East Indian derivation.

Chat—Officers' term for cootie; supposed to be more delicate.

Click—Variously used. To die. To be killed. To kill. To draw some disagreeable job, as: I clicked a burial fatigue.

Communication trench—A trench leading up to the front trench.

Consolidate—To turn around and prepare for occupation a captured trench.

Cootie—The common,—the too common,—body louse. Everybody has 'em.

Crater—A round pit made by an underground explosion or by a shell.

Cushy—Easy. Soft.

Dixie—An oblong iron pot or box fitting into a field kitchen. Used for cooking anything and everything. Nobody seems to know why it is so called.

Doggo—Still. Quiet. East Indian derivation.

Doing in—Killing.

Doss—Sleep.

Duck walk—A slatted wooden walk in soft ground.

Dud—An unexploded shell. A dangerous thing to fool with.

Dug-out—A hole more or less deep in the side of a trench where soldiers are supposed to rest.

Dump—A place where supplies are left for distribution.

Entrenching tool—A sort of small shovel for quick digging. Carried as part of equipment.

Estaminet—A French saloon or cafe.

Fag—A cigarette.

Fatigue—Any kind of work except manning the trenches.

Fed up—Tommy's way of saying "too much is enough."

Firing step—A narrow ledge running along the parapet on which a soldier stands to look over the top.

Flare—A star light sent up from a pistol to light up out in front.

Fritz—An affectionate term for our friend the enemy.

Funk hole—A dug-out.

Gas—Any poisonous gas sent across when the wind is right. Used by both sides. Invented by the Germans.

Goggles—A piece of equipment similar to that used by motorists, supposed to keep off tear gas. The rims are backed with strips of sponge which Tommy tears off and throws the goggle frame away.

Go west—To die.

Grouse—Complain. Growl. Kick.

Hun—A German.

Identification disc—A fiber tablet bearing the soldier's name, regiment, and rank. Worn around the neck on a string.

Iron rations—About two pounds of nonperishable rations to be used in an emergency.

Knuckle knife—A short dagger with a studded hilt. Invented by the Germans.

Lance Corporal—The lowest grade of non-commissioned officer.

Lewis gun—A very light machine gun invented by one Lewis, an officer in the American army.

Light railway—A very narrow-gauge railway on which are pushed little hand cars.

Listening post—One or more men go out in front, at night, of course, and listen for movements by the enemy.

Maconochie—A scientifically compounded and well-balanced ration, so the authorities say. It looks, smells, and tastes like rancid lard.

M.O.—Medical Officer. A foxy cove who can't be fooled with faked symptoms.

Mess tin—A combination teapot, fry pan, and plate.

Military cross—An officer's decoration for bravery.

Military medal—A decoration for bravery given to enlisted men.

Mills—The most commonly used hand grenade.

Minnies—German trench mortar projectiles.

Napper—The head.

Night 'ops—A much hated practice manoeuvre done at night.

No Man's Land—The area between the trenches.

On your own—At liberty. Your time is your own.

Out or over there—Somewhere in France.

Parados—The back wall of a trench.

Parapet—The front wall of a trench.

Patrol—One or more men who go out in front and prowl in the dark, seeking information of the enemy.

Periscope—A boxlike arrangement with two mirrors for looking over the top without exposing the napper.

Persuader—A short club with a nail-studded head.

Pip squeak—A German shell which makes that kind of noise when it comes over.

Push up the daisies—To be killed and buried.

Ration party—A party of men which goes to the rear and brings up rations for the front line.

Rest—Relief from trench service. Mostly one works constantly when "resting."

Ruddy—Same as bloody, but not quite so bad.

Sandbag—A bag which is filled with mud and used for building the parapet.

Sentry go—Time on guard in the front trench, or at rest at headquarters.

Shell hole—A pit made by the explosion of a shell.

Souvenir—Any kind of junk picked up for keepsakes. Also used as a begging word by the French children.

Stand to—Order for all men to stand ready in the trench in event of a surprise attack, usually at sundown and sunrise.

Stand down—Countermanding "stand to."

Stokes—A bomb weighing about eleven pounds usually thrown from a mortar, but sometimes used by hand.

Strafing—One of the few words Tommy has borrowed from Fritz. To punish.

Suicide club—The battalion bombers.

Tin hat—Steel helmet.

Wave—A line of men going over the top.

Whacked—Exhausted. Played out.

Whiz-bang—A German shell that makes that sort of noise.

Wind up or windy—Nervous. Jumpy. Temporary involuntary fear.

Wooden cross—The small wooden cross placed over a soldier's grave.

Image 1. *British soldiers at chow in the trenches* (1918) [Photograph] At: http://www.gwpda.org/photos/coppermine/displayimage .php?album=13&pos=415

Lightning Source UK Ltd.
Milton Keynes UK
UKHW010735180419
341238UK00002B/601/P

9 781473 314597